The Trophy Effect

Destroying Self-Doubt, Discovering Your True Self, and Taking Control of Your Life Forever!

By

Michael A. Nitti

Foreword by Noah St. John

The Trophy Effect

by
Michael A. Nitti

Published by Motivational Press, Inc.
7668 El Camino Real, #104-223
Carlsbad, CA 92009

ISBN: 9780982575536

Written by Michael A. Nitti

Publisher: Motivational Press, Inc
7668 El Camino Real, #104-223
Carlsbad, CA 92009

www.MotivationalPress.com

For information about custom editions, special sales, premium and corporate purchases, please contact Motivational Press Special Sales Department at 888-357-4441.

The Trophy Effect

Destroying Self-Doubt, Discovering Your True Self, and Taking Control of Your Life Forever!

* *

"*The Trophy Effect will change your life.* I know, because it changed the life of someone very near and dear to me – for which I am eternally grateful. This is ground-breaking work; an incredible journey you will never forget..."

-Dr. Tony Alessandra, Author: "The Platinum Rule"
Member of the Speakers Hall of Fame

"*The Trophy Effect rocks!* This is the ultimate Self-help tool and the best exercise I've ever seen – and I've seen them all! Thank you, Michael, for making this simple, yet powerful, process available to all of those who are controlled by their (mostly unconscious) fears. Nothing can stop me now! I'm on fire!! It's an absolutely brilliant approach – and I sincerely hope that millions of people will read this book and transform their lives forever!!"

-T. J. Rohleder, Author ("America's Blue Jeans Millionaire")

"A profound and courageous work. Your life will truly never be the same. Michael Nitti has developed a technique to master the inner-workings of the human mind; revealing a sustainable life of complete satisfaction and limitless possibility. Decades of personal study and practical exercise uphold the message and lessons contained in this book. Michael gifts us a missing piece of the puzzle, allowing us to become the masters of our fate and the captains of our soul. A journey inward you do not want to miss..."

-David Morehouse, PhD; Author: "The Psychic Warrior"

"Having retired at age thirty-nine, I soon found myself asking "is this all there is to life?" Fortunately, it wasn't too long before I was introduced to Michael Nitti and discovered the secret of *The Trophy Effect* – and along with it, my true "Self." I was inspired to step beyond my fears and to launch what has grown into yet another successful business - and am now teaching *The Trophy Effect* to my clients as well. Therefore, here's my coaching; "The Trophy Effect" is incredible. Read it now and change your life forever!"

-Tim Taylor, Real Estate Mentor & Success Coach
www.timtaylorsuccesscoach.com

To Julie…

"I love you with all my heart"

--- DEDICATION ---

"The mind asks the questions, the heart has the answers."
-Byron Katie

This book is dedicated to those who possess
the desire to know the truth as well as the courage
to not be dissuaded by the elusive nature of that truth –
for they are our future teachers.

To those who are willing to embrace what they do not
know and who remain undeterred in the absence of any
promise as to when they may come to know it –
for they shall become our greatest teachers.

I dedicate this book to all the teachers and all the students
and I honor all those who learn with the intent to teach.
Therefore, in celebration of what you are about to learn –
I honor that in *you,* which is also in *me*
and I am grateful for the opportunity to be
your teacher on this journey…

Namaste.

---

*"Those who bring sunshine to the lives of others
cannot keep it from themselves."*
-Sir James Barrie

To Werner…

"The source of my experience"

- - - ACKNOWLEDGMENTS - - -

"Keep away from people who try to belittle your ambitions. Small people always do that, but the really great make you feel that you, too, can become great as well..."

-Mark Twain

Over the course of the twenty-five years that I have been contemplating *The Trophy Effect*, I am blessed to have been inspired by a host of brilliant teachers and an abundance of amazing clients; all of whom have contributed more than they could possibly know to the writing of this book. To all of those who have shared their truth and impacted my life so profoundly, I am eternally grateful.

Specifically, I am privileged to have met and to have participated in course work the following individuals; each of whom I consider mentors and whose work has become my work: Tony Robbins, Deepak Chopra, Wayne Dyer, Werner Erhard, and Gangaji.

To my Father, Dominick Nitti, an original "Navy Seal" (UDT 11), who served both his country during WW II and his family, with honor– and to whom I promised just before he passed away that I would write this book. To my mother, Vivian, who, during her fifty-five year partnership with my father, stood proudly at his side, which I appreciate more than can be told. To my sisters Sharon, Diann, and Paula, who were the first females to demonstrate to me the magnificence of the feminine spirit. To my wife, Julie, who I am exceptionally privileged to have called my lover for over twenty years. She is *truly* special. To Julie's mother and step father, Jinx and Ed, whom I love with all my heart. To my extended families, including

Julie's father, Bill, her brother Rusty and his family, as well as each of my sister's families; I will always cherish our times together! To my daughters, on whom I "practiced transformation" as kids (and who have blossomed into amazing souls, so it must have worked) and their husbands; Erica and Steve, and Amy and Howie – I love you all more than you can know…

To Steve Curtis, for his amazing friendship and for being a living example of how it is possible to achieve *anything* you focus on – as well as our mutual friend and fellow coach, Tim Taylor, who played a major role in this book coming to fruition. To all of my closest friends, who knew what I was up to and who "made sure that I had fun" during the process, especially Laura and Craig Burness and Patty and David Morehouse, as well as Lyn and Sam Georges, who are responsible for me being in San Diego and coming to work with the Robbins organization in the first place. I am forever grateful.

To my exceptionally close friend, Faith Gorski, who is *always* there no matter what; your friendship truly inspires me and lightens my heart.

To those who coached me or otherwise played a key role in my own transformation, specifically Laurel Scheaf, Angelo D'milio, Randy McNamara, Jan Cook, David Norris, David Fisher, Doug Gouge, Patricia Johnson, and Toba Hettleman – as well as those with whom I've worked and have known to act selflessly in support of *Robbins Research* out of their commitment to transform the lives of others, specifically: Pam and Chris Hendrickson, Shari Wilson, Mary Glorfield, Lucas Johnson, Jacqueline Cornaby, Susie Conine, Gary Schwertly, Cloe Madanes; PhD, and Deb Flores (you will be missed), as well as Joseph McClendon III, who was kind enough to coach me with regard to this manuscript. I also thank the following Robbins personnel, who supported me behind the scenes; Reggie Batts, Brett Williams, Tommy Dones, Janet O'dea, and Joy Nored.

To Annie Reuter, who was originally referred to me as a client and has since become a special friend – and who supported me immensely with the creation of this book, as well as Carole Harvey, another "client turned friend," who has provided both amazing insight and editing support along the way. With regard to those who provided their professional expertise and guidance in support of the publication of this book, I acknowledge Noah St. John, Dr. Tony Alessandra, Janet Switzer, Vicki St. George, Ann McIndoo, and Justin Sachs. Thank you for enabling me to manifest this dream!

To the many clients who permitted me to lead them through *The Trophy Effect* and then allowed it to empower them, thereby demonstrating both its effectiveness and their personal courage, specifically: Shariq Thanvi, Sandy Dresser, Dr. Shelley Cathrea, Ian Aplin, Jeff Gardner, Mark Biddlecombe, Robert Antonicello, Oralia Rojas, Joanna Lamarra, Louise Huusom, Casper Pedersen, Jette Nielsen, Rob and Diana Linton, Jeannie Catchpole, Dana and Greg Thornton, Dr. Aleksandra Drecun, Kimberly Acworth, Zofia Syrek, Mustafa Abbas, Juliann Kovan, Sue Walker, Jacob and Maria Morrow, Londina Cruz, Abe Tatosian, Chris Niphakis, Mia Gyzander, Johnny Costa, Dr. Kwan Jakobsen, Karen Chilton, Craig Bradshaw, Mike Stamos, Todd Isberner, T.J. Rohleder, Andrew DeCurtis, Jessica Alessandra, Karissa Moreland, Dr. Julie Royal, Kevin Walker, Maggie Kestly, Theresa Lombardi, Dr. Michael Sasevich, Gino Scialdone, Chris Sutliff, and Mandy and Matthew Mushlin (the "Trophy King"), among many others – but especially Pernille and her team at Mindjuice.dk; I am truly inspired by you all!

Finally, I acknowledge *you*, the reader, for your willingness to open your mind and for your intention to discover your true *Self*…

Enjoy the ride…

"We cannot discover new oceans until we have the courage to lose sight of the shore."

-Muriel Chen

"The Trophy Effect"

TABLE *of* CONTENTS

"Before we can learn, we need to learn how to learn,
and before we can learn how to learn, we need to unlearn."

-Sufi aphorism

- - - FOREWORD - - -

Yes, you made the *right* decision. The right decision to read this book. No matter how you came to know about *The Trophy Effect,* you'll soon be very glad you did.

When my friend, real estate mentor Tim Taylor, told me that he had just produced a major breakthrough in his business (and his life) as a result of participating in something he called *"The Trophy Effect,"* I assumed that he had recently attended yet another personal growth seminar.

However, as he continued to explain how he had been thoroughly transformed by the experience, I was surprised to discover that he had spent little more than an hour with author and life coach Michael Nitti, who had walked him through *The Trophy Effect* process by phone. And although I was happy to learn of his breakthrough, I also recall wondering how something so impactful could have happened in "little more than an hour" – so I asked Tim that very question.

"You'll find out soon enough," he smiled; which was his way of saying that he had already convinced Michael to lead me through *The Trophy Effect* process the following week. "In fact," he added, "I knew you'd be impressed, so I promised him you'd help him with his book!"

If you're familiar with my book, *The Secret Code of Success*, you know that I've always been fascinated by the question: "Why does success seem to come so naturally to a few, while the rest seem to struggle all their lives?"

In my quest to answer this question, I am blessed to have shared what I've learned with tens of thousands of clients and readers around the world. I've made it my business to tell the difference between something that is merely "interesting" and that which is "truly profound" – which is why I can assure you that what you are about to experience is *very* profound.

You see, when Michael finally walked me through *The Trophy Effect* on the phone, it had an immediate impact on my life and the way I look at nearly every situation I encounter. What's more, it has continued to make a difference from that moment on, as I am constantly reminded of the power of *The Trophy Effect* at every turn.

In fact, one of the most powerful aspects of *The Trophy Effect* is the journey itself, which Michael has designed specifically to allow you to *experience* what you are reading rather than simply "understand" it – thereby enabling you to embrace and apply every distinction as fully as possible.

As you observe these distinctions, you'll begin to perceive both your Self and your circumstances in a remarkable new light, leaving you fully empowered to live *intentionally* rather than *in reaction* to those circumstances. Ultimately, you will be invited to venture beyond *The Trophy Effect* toward an even higher level of consciousness, which I believe you'll find to be a very enlightening culmination to a magnificent journey!

Just as my friend promised, I was impressed, as well as inspired, by *The Trophy Effect* – and as you can see, I kept my promise to help Michael with this book!

Wishing you all the love and happiness you deserve, I give you – *The Trophy Effect...*

Enjoy!

Noah St. John

Author of ***The Secret Code of Success***
www.SuccessClinic.com

"The Trophy Effect"

by

Michael A. Nitti

- - - INTRODUCTION - - -

Welcome to *The Trophy Effect.* I'm honored that you bought this book.

Now, please do yourself a favor and don't read it.

If you do, all that you'll get is *smarter* – yet that is not the purpose of this book. You are already smart. I didn't write it with the intention of making you smarter.

You see, if you simply read this book expecting to *learn* about *The Trophy Effect,* that's precisely what will happen. You will simply learn about it – just as you've learned about other things that have made very little difference in your life.

The purpose of this book is to make a difference. A difference in how you *feel.*

You are about to embark on a journey that has the power to both lighten your heart and strengthen your sense of purpose. A journey designed to enliven you and to leave you feeling even more exuberant than you felt as a child; a feeling that nothing can stop you from designing and living the life of your dreams.

During this journey, we will be observing and examining the inner workings of your psychology from a totally unique perspective; free of the preconceived notions and cultural influences that normally alter how you and I perceive things.

In support of this examination, I will be asking you to keep both a journal and an open mind – so please keep both. I will also be asking that you think back on your life and to recall certain incidents, so please allow yourself to visualize whatever comes to mind and then make note of what you see in your journal.

You will also notice that I sometimes re-state or reemphasize specific points, which are vital to the outcome. Therefore, when I point to a consideration from multiple perspectives, please allow for this as a critical means to an end – and, in the end, you will understand.

Ultimately, I will be leading you through a series of incredibly powerful exercises, which – in spite of the fact that they are also incredibly simple – have the power to transform your life forever. In light of which, I suggest that you play full out and settle for nothing less!

Finally, I invite you to enjoy this journey and know that if you expect *The Trophy Effect* to make a difference, it will. And, if it also happens to make you smarter, you'll simply have to live with that…

"He who knows others is wise. He who knows himself is enlightened."

-Lao Tzu

"The Trophy Effect"

Destroying Self-Doubt, Discovering Your True Self, and Taking Control of Your Life Forever!

Chapter 1 - *Life in a Fishbowl*

"What a dummy!"

"How stupid was that?"

"I can't believe I did that *again!!*"

Sound familiar? If so, fess up – how often do you find yourself having thoughts like these after doing something wrong or foolish or after making a simple mistake? How many times a day do you catch yourself either wondering if you are *good enough* with respect to a specific task at hand or doubting yourself as the result of reflecting negatively upon something that may have happened days, weeks, or even *years* ago? In fact, have you ever noticed that no matter how many great things you or I accomplish, we are much more likely to beat ourselves up when things go wrong than we are to congratulate ourselves when things go right?

In which case, one might wonder, what's up with that?

Then again, one may not be inclined to wonder about that at all, as I am suggesting that we have grown so accustomed to worrying about "not being good enough" that we've become just like the proverbial fish who has no clue that it's surrounded by water; the premise being that having spent its entire life in water, the fish has no alternative perspective from which to experience the water *as water*. Sort of like not being able to see the forest for the trees…

No matter how intelligent, capable, or successful we may be, if most of us were brutally honest about it, we would admit to questioning either our capabilities or our self worth on a fairly regular basis – or, at least whenever things go wrong – and can easily recall the last time we were present to a thought such as "damn, that was stupid."

In fact, this tendency to catch ourselves *not* measuring up is so strong, that even if you had just graduated from a major university, married the man or woman of your dreams, or were standing in front of an audience being lauded by your peers, there's a very good chance that you wouldn't allow yourself to feel too good about it nor allow any praise to sink in too deeply. So, what is this "subconscious force" that causes us to feel validated when we do something wrong, yet relatively resistant to positive validation when we do something well?

In the interest of cutting right to the chase, the bottom line is that you and I are not "wired" to expect things to go our way. You see, even in the wake of the buzz about the "Law of Attraction" and all of the books that implore us to think only positive thoughts, this is *not* how human beings are put together. In fact, we are much more likely to be concerned about falling short than we are inclined to anticipate success.

Certainly, there are those of us who achieve our goals and do great things every day, as each of us is fully capable of accomplishing whatever outcome we desire by moving toward it with focus, intention, and determination. However, since most of us do not appear to be able to generate this level of intention on a regular basis nor bring forth that degree of determination as a matter of course, wouldn't it be useful to discover what it is that keeps us from doing so? Wouldn't it serve us to acknowledge the truth about those recurring tendencies that cause us to hesitate or hold back? Might it not be liberating to discover the source of the self-doubt that tends to show up whenever we consider taking action in pursuit of something we desire? Furthermore, wouldn't it be interesting to observe how our minds are *really* wired so that we could assume fuller control over the "steering wheel" of our lives? Finally, wouldn't it be beneficial to understand these natural tendencies and compulsions so that we're able to have more power over *them* than they have over *us*?

Of course it would. And now that you've answered "yes" to each of these questions, I'm pleased to inform you that there exists a similarly simple answer to the fundamental question behind those posed above – and that question is "what is preventing us from having it all?" In fact, it's an answer so simple that you may actually feel like you've fallen short once again because you should have figured it out for yourself. Still, whether you've figured it out or not, the reason why we feel validated when we come up short yet resist feeling joyful when we don't, is: Fear. Yes, *fear*. Not just any fear, mind you, but a fear so strong that it drives *all* of our self-doubt, *all* of our hesitation, and *all* of our justification for giving up rather than staying the course in pursuit of our dreams. So, what specifically might it be that we are so afraid of that it causes us to question almost everything we do?

Well, although he's not the only authority on human nature to acknowledge the role that fear plays in our lives, as is a recurring theme throughout many of his ground-breaking works, my friend and mentor, Tony Robbins, has concluded that there are two fundamental human fears, 1) *that we are not enough*, and 2) *that we will not be loved.* These being the observations of a man whose teachings have impacted the lives of millions of human beings!

Basically, what Tony is suggesting is that no matter where we go or what we set out to accomplish, these fears go along for the ride. Of course, we rarely observe these fears for what they are for the very same reason that the fish isn't able to *see* the water (again, the premise being that the fish has no alternative perspective from which to experience the water *as water*, having spent its entire life in it). Even so, these fears are definitely there – lurking just beneath the surface, patiently awaiting the announcement of your next big dream or intention so that they can intervene and cause you to re-think everything. At which point, what exactly are your options for breaking free of these fears?

As you can imagine, there is no simple answer. However, we will be exploring this question from two very distinct perspectives, as it is my intention that by the time you've finished reading this book, you'll have mastered breaking free of these fears from both a "traditional" and a *transformed* point-of-view.

From either perspective, any such breakthrough will require a thorough understanding of *The Trophy Effect.* And since that just happens to be the subject of this book, you're off to a very promising start – as we begin with a fairly traditional analysis…

First of all, with respect to how our fundamental fears come into play within this dynamic, I've observed that the concern of not being good enough is our *primary* fear, which then spawns a virtual smorgasbord of secondary fears. Being privileged to have coached more than a thousand clients one-on-one over the past twenty-five years (as well as having witnessed Tony interacting live with hundreds of thousands of others during seven of those years), I can assure you that I've never met anyone who doesn't exhibit at least some degree of limiting behavior stemming from these fears; specifically, the primary fear of not being good enough.

As for those of you who may be resisting this little piece of news (either because you don't believe you have these fears or because you don't believe you allow them to stop you), please understand that although these fears exist, most of us have built "mental muscles" that allow us to make things happen in spite of them – at least *some* of the time.

Consequently, since it's true that all human beings share these fears, yet most of us still produce outcomes and ultimately create at least some degree of prosperity in our lives, what we're about to explore – and ultimately overcome – is how these fears significantly limit your vision, thwart your determination, rob you of your self-esteem and enthusiasm, and dampen your sense of fulfillment.

Even then, understanding how we are affected by these fears is only the first step, as my primary objective in writing this book is to leave each reader fully empowered to dream grander dreams and to move toward them with renewed confidence and passion!

You see, the truth really does set one free; so, if you are willing to surrender into what is about to be revealed – as we explore what we're about to explore – what is available on the other side of this journey is anything your heart desires!

On the other hand, if you already have everything your heart desires or are still not clear about how the fear of not being good enough has impacted your life, I encourage you to keep looking until you are able to see both the "water" in your *personal fishbowl* and that it's not just all the other "fish" who seem to be affected by these fears. Once you do, I suggest that you continue this journey as a *full participant* rather than as an observer. After all, no matter how conscious you may be, what can it hurt to discover something you didn't know – the knowing of which might support you in becoming even more empowered and joyful than you already are?

With this in mind, I invite you to continue reading as though what lies hidden within these pages is nothing less than the secret formula for freedom, happiness, and fulfillment! I further invite you to "try everything on" for yourself by looking into your experience to discover how each metaphor applies to you; knowing that you are much more likely to become enlightened if you read with the intent to *align* rather than *doubt.*

Surely, it would be easy for your mind to dismiss some of what you are about to read as too general. And although we do, in fact, possess unique personalities, we clearly share the same "basic operating system," which lies at the root of how we interpret and process information. And it is here – at the level of this operating system – where you and I are very much alike; exhibiting the same emotions, the same access to memories, the same survival instinct, and the same *fears*.

Of course, on a much more fundamental level, we are not only "very much alike," but are inextricably connected to everyone and everything else, *as one.* However, this aspect is typically far less ascertainable for a myriad of reasons – primarily because all of us have been "socially conditioned" to trust our perceptions (our senses) rather than conduct our own investigation into the true nature of things. Thus, in order to actually *experience* "oneness" and to celebrate the joy of our inherent connectedness, we must first understand the very nature of social conditioning itself. Which, conveniently, is both a very crucial aspect of *The Trophy Effect* and one that we're about to explore first hand.

Therefore, my final invitation is for you to use this process to conduct your *own* investigation, thereby enabling you to let go of any limiting beliefs that have been tied to your social (and personal) conditioning. In the end, you will learn how to "recondition" both your mind and the actual *neural-connectors* within your brain – at which point, you will be fully empowered to step beyond your fishbowl and to experience yourself as the magnificent and capable being you truly are!

In support of all this, we are about to embark on a relatively simple, yet very powerful, metaphorical journey through the inner workings of *the mind.* A journey which has been structured to allow you to see that we are not only influenced by these forces but are driven by them – and why we so often feel like we don't measure up. A journey of exploration and observation, where there's a very good chance that you'll be seeing things as you've never seen them before – at least not from *outside* the fishbowl.

Needless to say, you're in for quite a ride. So, let's fasten our seat belts and get this show on the road!

Chapter 2 - *The Journey Begins*

Let us begin by taking a moment to once more acknowledge our fundamental fears – *that we are not enough, that we may not be good enough, and that we will somehow fall short.* Again, these are *innate* fears. This is how we are wired. In other words, these fears not only represent the water inside our fishbowl, these fears are our fishbowl…

Having observed that we are driven by these fears, let us now assume that we are swimming around inside this metaphorical fishbowl; the one in which we co-exist with this ever-present concern about not being good enough. In which case, wouldn't it follow that *everything* we experience would be perceived through the filter of this fear? In fact, wouldn't this dynamic also explain why you and I tend to wonder not *if,* but *when* it's all going to fall apart even when we do succeed or achieve a significant outcome?

After all, in the shadow of this subconscious concern that you aren't good enough, wouldn't any success show up as having been arbitrarily achieved *in spite of* this fear rather than as evidence that you *are* good enough?

Another question: What is it that you and I do when we're concerned about something? We pay it extra attention, right? We stand guard. We remain alert "just in case."

You see, when we're afraid of something, we are *compelled* to be on the lookout for that very thing. This is how the mind works. It's a good thing (when it is), as this is one of the ways the mind achieves its purpose of ensuring our safety – our *survival*.

So, in the face of this innate fear that you're not good enough, what are you likely to be searching for at every turn? What would you tend to be looking for on a moment-by-moment basis? Absolutely! *Proof* that you're not good enough!! Actually, you and I have very little control over this process, as this is simply the mind doing its job – which is to ensure our survival by watching out for *anything* that might do us harm.

Consider this: If you were to tell a four year old that there's a monster in his closet, what would he be looking for every time he opens the door? You got it – a monster. Because when we're afraid of something, it's only natural for us to be on the lookout for it.

How about this one: If a woman is concerned that her lover is cheating on her (which, for many women, is a very real fear), and then one day he comes home wearing a brand new cologne, what does this mean? That's right. Proof that he is cheating. And why? Because her *fear* is driving her to be on the lookout for *any* proof that she may be right! And if he should empty his pockets and she notices a piece of paper with a phone number on it? Exactly. Further proof – and for the same reason.

Of course, could the mind be wrong about either of these assumptions? Absolutely, as the man may have simply decided to try a new fragrance. And we all know that the phone number could have belonged to just about anyone other than a new lover. In any case, what's important to notice here is that it's not the mind's job to determine what's accurate and what isn't, as the mind can't afford to take any chances when survival is at stake!

In fact, the mind can pretty much be counted on to "react first and ask questions later," as its foremost objective is to ensure your survival at all costs (an instinct typically referred to by psychologists as "fight or flight" or "reaction"). Therefore, the mind doesn't care if it causes you or anyone else any upset or if it makes a mistake – as its principal inclination is to protect you from *anything* that might do you harm.

Hence, from a functional perspective, ***survival*** is the primary purpose of the mind. And although our minds are able to perform all sorts of other neat tricks, if you look into your own experience, you will observe that survival is the primary purpose of the mind in all animal species.

When the mind of *any* animal perceives a threat, what does it do?

Well, without hesitating to consider whether the threat is real or not, it immediately burrows into the ground, climbs a tree, takes off running, changes color, spits, attacks, hisses – or whatever! What the mind doesn't do is wait around to see if it made a mistake.

Significantly, the human mind operates in precisely the same fashion, which means that it is consistently on the lookout for anything we fear and will take prompt and effective action once it detects a threat – such as whenever it perceives that we are about to fail, about to be wrong, or about to appear foolish. When this happens, the mind takes complete control over our body, at which point, we are pretty much being taken for a ride.

More than likely, you've witnessed this "cause and effect" dynamic, which is commonly referred to as "being in survival." Someone "goes off" (or, conversely, "closes down") and, in the absence of any obvious regard for the consequences, that individual is fully and undeniably "in survival"; saying or doing things we know they are going to regret later – as this survival instinct is a very powerful force. Unfortunately, when *survival* takes over our thinking, it can also get us into powerful trouble.

I can *feel* you thinking – so let's pause here to address some of the more obvious questions you may have at this point:

1) What the heck is *"The Trophy Effect"* and what does all of this stuff about survival have to do with it?

2) I can appreciate this explanation of "survival" and can see how it applies *some* of the time – yet if this is the purpose of the mind, then why don't we react like this *all* of the time – like animals seem to do?

3) Is it really true that fish don't know they are in water?

Great questions! Here's what you need to know for now...

1) I'll be explaining *The Trophy Effect* very soon (although everything you've read thus far is part of the process), so please hang in there.
2) The reason we do not react out of survival *every* time we perceive a threat is because we are sometimes able to shift into an *intentional* state of "Being" (or "Self") from which we consciously choose to override the mind, thereby generating an *intentional* response to the perceived threat rather than a *reactionary* response. However, as you've probably noticed, this is a relatively rare and random occurrence for most human beings. Yet, you and I absolutely possess the ability to consciously shift from *reaction* into *intention* at any given moment!

So, if each of us is able to override "reaction" by initiating an *intentional* response to a perceived threat, then why don't we do so more often?

Well, because the *default* mechanism of the mind is always survival! Which means the mind is *always* on the lookout for threats. Thus, whenever a threat is detected, the mind *always* sends a signal to our body to take evasive action, which *always* results in the mind initiating a survival response. So, unless the Self intervenes, the mind instinctively *reacts* – at which point we have very little control over what we say or do.

Now, besides fear, the reasons why we don't override the survival response more often are considerable and include: personal conditioning (habit), low self-esteem or lack of confidence, apathy, resignation (or depression), or, as is often the case, the simple lack of an intention or a purpose for doing so. Not only that, but the mind absolutely *hates* being questioned, *refuses* to lose, *detests* being wrong, *resists* being dominated, and *must feel justified* at every turn; especially when defending our (its) point-of-view.

And so the mind waits – and if and when any such threat appears (which is likely to occur countless times per day), it takes over!

As you can see, *the mind* pretty much has *the Self* hemmed in. Yet, the odds against the Self breaking through are even more insurmountable because there are two even greater reasons why we don't "live from intention" on a more regular basis, which are:

a) The mind's will to survive us is so strong that it actually perceives any intervention from the Self as just another threat! Thus, even when we do initiate an intention to override the mind, the minds interpretation is that we are about to make a big mistake in not trusting it to survive us through the imminent threat. In response, it steps up its resistance to the Self, thereby initiating a sort of *tug-of-war* between "survival" and "intention." At this point, it's a crapshoot as to which force wins out, yet I assure you that the Self will win only if we are focused on a compelling outcome and move toward it with intention and determination.

b) Lack of awareness – in that most of us are simply not conscious of the fact that we can choose to override the mind by acting *intentionally*. After all, how many times have you had this survival dynamic explained to you in this manner? The simple truth is that most of us spend the majority of our time *in survival* because we have never identified with the "Self," nor have we ever defined an option called "living with intention." For the vast majority of us, these truths have been obscured by the whirlpool of fear and doubt swirling around within our fishbowl.

However, from now on you *will* be aware, so you *will* have a choice.

3) True; fish do not know they are in water, except for Flying Fish, which are magically transformed and enlightened the moment they push through their fears and take that very first leap into the unknown!

Now, what about *you?*

Whether or not you've contemplated these concepts before, the dynamics we've discussed thus far are relatively complex and can be confusing; so, to ensure that you're "getting it," I've prepared a little quiz. And although it's important that you pass this quiz before reading any further, I predict you'll do just fine. In any case, please don't skip over it – and have fun…

Multiple choice (in case you couldn't tell):

1) Fish do *not* know:
    a) Enough to keep them from being eaten by larger fish
    b) That they taste better with a little butter and parsley
    c) That they are swimming in water
2) Human Beings all share these same fundamental fears:
    a) That we will forget where we left our keys and then we'll be late
    b) That we won't find a decent parking space and then we'll be late
    c) That we are not good enough and won't be loved
3) The primary purpose of the mind is:
    a) Remembering where we left our keys
    b) Coming up with excuses for why we were late
    c) Survival
4) To break free of the tug-of-war between *Survival* and *Self* we must:
    a) Observe it occurring and know that we have the ability to choose
    b) Intentionally over-ride the minds compulsion to survive our point-of-view
    c) Create outcomes and move toward them with courage and determination
    d) All of the above

5) If a man shows up wearing a new cologne, it obviously means that:
    a) He is cheating on his wife or girlfriend
    b) You should search his pocket for a piece of paper with a phone number on it
    c) You really don't know. Yet at least he smells better, so let it go

So, how'd you do? I know, it wasn't that difficult – primarily because I plugged all of the correct answers into the (c) spot; except, of course, for number (4), where I thought I'd take advantage of an opportunity to emphasize a few key points. In any case, please observe that once your mind was convinced that the third answer was likely to be the correct answer, it enjoyed noticing whether or not this pattern was going to be repeated.

You see, the mind *lives* for this sort of thing. It loves to predict what is going to happen based on what has happened *before.* In fact, this is one of the ways in which the mind carries out its mission to survive us – by looking at how it survived us *in the past* and then doing that same thing again. After all, why not? Even the mind has no interest in re-inventing the wheel. In any case, please file this little piece of information away, as I promise it will come in handy later on. Until then, on with the journey…

"Every time you are tempted to react in the same old way, ask if you want to be a prisoner of the past or a pioneer of the future."

–Deepak Chopra

Notes -

Chapter 3 - *The Daisy Chain Dilemma*

Okay, who's prepared to earn themselves some Trophies? Or, if asked more accurately, who's prepared to discover that they've been earning Trophies all along? Hopefully, you're ready, because the time has come for us to explore what ***The Trophy Effect*** is all about. It's time to discover how this dynamic has played an enormous role in your life forever – and how, once understood and harnessed, it can have an even more profound and positive effect on your future!

However, it is essential that you first embrace everything you've learned about our *primary fears* and *survival* before moving forward. For in order to fully appreciate the impact that *The Trophy Effect* has had on our lives, we must accept the premise that we do, in fact, share our fishbowls with both ***the fear of not being good enough*** and a tremendously strong compulsion ***to survive*** (to react instinctively in favor of) ***our personal point of view*** (which is why I included that little quiz in the previous chapter). Even so, please be certain that I have no desire to force these beliefs upon you – however, if you've not yet grasped these basic concepts, I suggest that you review the first two chapters "until they sink in."

Frankly, if you've found it difficult to accept either of these premises – particularly the assertion that so much of our daily life is affected by this subconscious "tug-of-war" between *survival* and *intention* – you are not alone. As previously inferred, the mind is not at all interested in you becoming conscious of this dynamic because such an awareness may prompt *the Self* to bring forth even more intention to override *the mind* more often – which befuddles the mind to no end – as it is simply attempting to do its job!

Given which, if you are having trouble grasping this concept, it's because the mind (which is also in charge of you understanding it), doesn't want you to understand it. Get it? It's kind of like having the key to a lockbox being locked *inside* the lockbox. Thus, once you do understand this dynamic, notice that you had to become sort of an "Intentional Houdini" in order to "get the key" so that you could "unlock the box." Therefore, if you have grasped this concept, I congratulate you and acknowledge your intention!

And now that you have picked this lock, let us continue…

First, however, allow me to shed even more light on the connection between our fundamental fears and our compulsion to survive them – which will support you in understanding why *The Trophy Effect* exists in the first place…

In her book, "Feel the Fear and Do it Anyway," Dr. Susan Jeffers suggests that if we intend to attain a desired outcome, our only viable option is to step beyond our fears to make it happen! To be sure, most of us do push through some degree of fear on a fairly regular basis. Yet rarely do we catch ourselves doing so, which is because we typically only push through ***itsy-bitsy*** fears – one itsy-bitsy fear at a time. In fact, if the mind had *its* way, you and I would simply "itsy-bitsy" our way through the rest of our lives! And although playing small is not likely to reward you with the life you deserve, at least you would feel very little pain, avoid every threat, and *survive!*

"Most of us tiptoe through life in order to make it safely to death."

–Theodore Roosevelt

Each of us has, indeed, built tiny muscles that allow us to break through *tiny* fears. However, bigger goals are sure to prompt *bigger* fears; at which point, depending upon how your mind sizes up the threat, it's bound to shift into *survival mode* and attempt to talk you out of it. Do you really want to subject yourself to all that embarrassment and humiliation? Do you really want to step beyond your comfort zone and take that risk?

What's important to note is that your mind is in no way opposed to you achieving your dreams. Yet, as we've learned, it is always going to steer you clear of any fear that it perceives as a threat (i.e., any situation where you could possibly *lose,* be *wrong,* be *dominated,* or be unable to *justify* any of it). Therefore, unless your desired outcome is so grand that you feel you must achieve it and your intention is so strong that it causes your Self to override your mind, we both know that you are not only likely to give up, but you are going to *remember* that you gave up!

What's worse, this very act of remembering unleashes a dynamic that causes us to instantly recall all of the other times we gave up or failed, thereby spawning our worst nightmare – a "lethal" combination of unpleasant memories, primary fears, and our compulsion to survive, which immediately "sucks the wind right out of us" and causes us to perceive everything worse than it is. A dynamic that causes us to take the smallest mistake and magnify it ten-fold! A dynamic that causes us to make mountains out of molehills – and then plants those mountains directly in our path!

And what is this dynamic that is able to wreak so much havoc on your psychology?

You guessed it: ***The Trophy Effect.***

> *"So, after all this, you are telling me that "The Trophy Effect" is a bad thing? I bought a self-help book about some "effect" that makes me feel like crap? Guess what! I think I'm feeling that effect right now!"*

Okay, remain calm. Yes, the *Trophy Effect* is responsible for *all* that is wrong in the world. However, that's only until you become aware of it, harness it, and then allow it to work *for* you rather than against you. As mentioned earlier, this is entirely possible – and probable – as shall be revealed later in our journey…

In the mean time – and continuing where we left off – imagine that you've established a meaningful outcome and begin to move toward it. As you are aware, this prompts you to feel fear – at which point, your mind perceives this as a threat and attempts to convince you to give up (which you now know that it does in order to survive you by preventing you from failing, losing, feeling foolish, etc.).

What is critical to note is that the mind is basing its advice to give up solely upon its concern that "you are not good enough to succeed," which, in part, was proven the *last time* you gave up.

Of course, you gave up that last time only because the mind convinced you to do so based upon a similar concern it had back then (i.e., you are not good enough to succeed), which had been proven the time before that because... *you gave up!* Of course, it convinced you to do so the time before that because it *already* had proof that you weren't good enough, which was based on the fact that you had quit the time before that, which was... well, you get it, right? Do you see what's going on here? Are you starting to smell the coffee?

Remember, the primary purpose of the mind is to survive you in the face of a threat. In this case, the threat/concern is that you might fail because you're not good enough to succeed – for which it has *tons* of proof. After all, you did give up, you did quit, and, what's more, you've done so countless times!

Again, it's not the mind's job to take anything else into consideration or to figure out why that happened. As with all other animals, its strongest inclination is to whisk you out of harm's way and it doesn't care if *it* makes a mistake or if you're not happy about it. Thus, the mind is totally oblivious to the fact that *it* caused the very situation from which it is drawing its proof that you're a quitter and not good enough to succeed! All it knows is that you keep doing it over and over again. In which case, you're not only a quitter, you must be pretty dumb!

Well, you're not dumb – you've simply been stuck firmly within the grasp of an annoying little sub-dynamic of *The Trophy Effect,* which I call the "Daisy Chain Dilemma."

Unfortunately, since each of us has a mind, it can't be avoided – and once we get caught up in this dynamic, there is essentially no way out! In fact, in the absence of any intention or input from the Self, we are destined to spend the rest of our lives going around and around in this vicious circle. Which is, I suggest, precisely what most of us have been doing…

Of course, now that you are aware of the Daisy Chain, you'll have the ability to observe it happening and will be able to step *beyond* it – yet this will require that you remain focused on an outcome and move toward it with intention – as the mind will always attempt to suck you back in and compel you to give up. After all, that's its job.

Okay, are you keeping up? I trust that you are, as we're about to dig in much deeper; deep into the inner workings of *The Trophy Effect.* Deep into the memory vaults of the mind where it has filed away all its *proof* that you and I aren't good enough. In fact, we are going in "with miners caps and pick axes," which is my way of suggesting that we're about to "get our hands dirty." We are about to *get real.* We are about to step into your mind in order to observe what is *really* going on – with the outcome of discovering exactly how *The Trophy Effect* causes us to think what we think and feel what we feel. We are about to witness it in action and then beat it at its own game!

As you can imagine, this is going to require that you be extra vigilant in following along. Therefore, although I've already invited you to remain fully engaged, doing so from this point forward is especially critical if you are intent on "getting" the result – which is nothing less than a full understanding of what has been keeping you mired in self-doubt and how to finally and fully attain all of the success and happiness you deserve!

In order to achieve this, I encourage you to follow all of the instructions and to allow yourself to surrender fully into the metaphor. I also suggest that when asked to ponder a question, you stop reading, answer it honestly, and then capture that answer on a notepad or in your journal. Look within yourself and discover *the truth.*

Frankly, this is a fairly simple process, yet it is also very powerful – or, at least it can be, if you simply follow my lead and do not allow *anything* to lead you astray…

Are you ready? Good, because we're going in...

Chapter 4 - *The Tour*

Well, here we are! Welcome to *your mind.*

Hopefully, you're enjoying the journey and have already learned some valuable lessons. Yet, as the saying goes, *"you ain't seen nothin' yet!"*

Our mission is very clear – and everything we have explored and learned thus far has prepared you for this moment and this purpose; to observe *The Trophy Effect* in action. We are here to witness first-hand how it all plays out. To "catch it red handed" on its own turf. To understand and acknowledge its power, yet marvel at its simplicity.

Yet, as we stand on the threshold of realizing this purpose, there is one more thing you should know – and that is the reason why I am guiding you through this process and for writing this book in the first place. You see, being able to recall a time when I was so depressed that I was unable to get out of bed for a month, I know very well what it's like to live in reaction to one's concern of not being good enough. I recall very clearly both the feelings of inadequacy and the belief that I had no control over my future – as well as a very real willingness to simply "itsy-bitsy myself" through the rest of my life…

Fortunately, that's not what I did – embarking instead upon a journey of self-discovery that ultimately awakened within me what is my intention that this book awaken in others. A journey that empowered me to break free of my fishbowl (which I never knew existed), thereby enabling me to live "on purpose." And, after having been transformed by the grace of that awakening some twenty-five years ago – I am now committing these words to paper with the intention of evoking a similar experience in *you!*

Simply put, my ultimate outcome in exposing *The Trophy Effect* is to enable you to shift from living *in reaction* to living *with intention.* For you to be able to feel and know that you have complete control over your life! This is why we are here. Why we learned about survival. Why we learned about the Daisy Chain. And why we're about to pass through a very important door. And, yet, why our journey has only just begun…

Certainly, I've poked at your mind – but all that's really happened thus far is that I've explained to you, the "*fish*," that I am about to lift you out of the water and have you look back down at it. You may be reading what I've written and may even understand the concept, but since you haven't done it yet, there's no tangible way of experiencing the impact. So, other than plenty of insight into survival and a lot of big build up, that's about all you've got, right? Exactly. In fact, all you should expect to feel right now is lots of anticipation and, perhaps, a little impatience; sort of like: *"show me the damn water already!"* If so, that's fine, as I'm simply checking in to make sure that you're all revved up and ready to go.

After all, it's not very often that one gets to take a tour of their own mind – which is why I encourage you to summon up all of your intention, dust off your visualization skills, and *play full out!*

Typically, if I were conducting this process live (either during a coaching session or in a workshop), this is where I'd have you close your eyes (in order to better visualize what I was saying). However, since you can't read with your eyes closed, you may find it easier to visualize what you're reading if you allow yourself to surrender into a more relaxed state of consciousness.

Therefore, I invite you to slip into this relaxed state even *now,* imagining that you are standing within an especially majestic, expansive, and peaceful space… further imagining that what you are envisioning is – *your mind.*

As you envision this space, I invite you to notice the absence of any activity – as well as the feeling of lightness and freedom within this very large "room" in which you and I are standing. Allow your-self to be present to the stillness. In fact, if we were to raise our voices at all, I'm pretty sure we'd hear an echo…

Now, imagine your-self coming full circle, envisioning a series of closed *doors* wrapped all the way around the perimeter of this room. Imagine as well that except for these doors, there's not much else to be seen. And yet, since it is a door that we're searching for, you're in the right place – as very soon we will not only find this door but will also step through it…

But first, there's something else I'd like to show you and some-one I'd like you to meet. Do you "see" that plain black curtain at the far side of the room? (At this point, you're supposed to say "yes" – so if you're resisting this process, I encourage you to *let go,* sharpen your visualization skills, and get with the program).

Good. I'm glad you see the curtain.

Now, as we begin walking towards this curtain (this is where you should be imagining yourself walking, so stay with me), I must warn you that we're not really supposed to go back there – as this area is typically off-limits to visitors. However, since this is *your* mind and *your* tour – and because you're here to learn all you can – I'll simply draw back this curt--

Damn! Have you ever seen a curtain pulled shut so quickly? Or heard *"Go Away!"* screamed any louder than that? Talk about react-ing out of survival! Sure proved my point about the echo, though, didn't it? In any case, let's not take it too personal, as it's pretty ob-vious that *someone* wasn't in the mood for visitors. Still, I do want you to see what's going on back there, so we'll definitely stop back later. Until then, let's move on and pay no more attention to that *little man* behind the curtain…

Pop Quiz! What is the "filter" through which human beings perceive *everything?*

a) That we are not good enough
b) That we have given up on things in the past, so we have *proof* that we're not good enough
c) That we've given up before and will likely do so again, so we are *definitely* not good enough!

Absolutely! You and I aren't good enough. And notice that you don't even have to contemplate these options *consciously*, because they are always being contemplated *for you* by your subconscious mind – so no matter how often your mind prompts you to consider these three options (which happens *every time* it perceives a threat) or which one you choose – you lose! Ironically, your mind actually recognizes this as "winning" because it gets to *be right* about what it already suspected to be true. What's more, this applies to all of us, for as long as we are human, we naturally have fear *"a,"* and thanks to the *Daisy Chain Dilemma*, we also have fears *"b"* and *"c."* Lucky us!

Alright – now that you've "passed" this little quiz, how about we find ourselves a door? Not just any door, of course, but *the* door. The one we came here to find. The one that's going to lead us out of survival and into *intention*...

So, back we go... allowing your-self to surrender into that relaxed state... settling back into that expansive space with all the doors – imagining yourself moving closer and closer to the perimeter of this room. As you envision yourself approaching these doors, I invite you to notice that some of them are not only larger than others, but are much nicer looking as well – leading you to observe that although many of them look like they've never been open, others appear to be worn and fairly well used. What's more, you will notice that all of these doors are closed right now...

Fortunately, on every door there's a sign – and on every sign there are words – which means that if we simply "read our way down the hall," we should have no trouble finding the one we're looking for – as we're about to arrive at the very first door…

And this one says - -

	Data Processing	Nope, that's not it.
-and this next one?	Short Term Memory	Important, but no.
-this one's larger:	Long Term Memory	Who'd have guessed? but nope.
-this one's cool:	Happy Memories	Very nice, but not now…
-here's a fun one:	Fantasies	Hey, let's take a peek! Was that a *no?*
-and this one?	Body Functions	Let's keep moving, shall we...
-this one's huge:	Mistakes	You're getting warmer...
-could this be it?	Bad Memories	Perhaps an overflow room, but *no.*
-ah, here we are…	The Trophy Room	*Bingo!*

We're here! Welcome to your *Trophy Room.*

Not a bad looking door, hey? Although it is pretty worn – especially at the bottom there – what are those? Kick marks? And you'll notice that it doesn't seem to shut all the way. Must be the lockset – it feels pretty loose. I'd say this door gets *plenty of use…*

Obviously, this door has seen better days. But then, it's not the door we came to see. It's what's on the other side. Even so, we're not going in just yet...

You see, what you are about to experience when we pass through this door is *the truth.* Yet, until I further explain why we're standing in front of this door or why you're about to step through it, it's unlikely that you'd find this room any more interesting – and certainly no more meaningful – than your broom closet.

Clearly, we've come a long way and you've already learned quite a lot – yet I'm not about to have you walk through this door too soon and unravel any of our hard work. I'm not at all interested in you hanging out in this room like some tourist.

Again, I'm not here to *tell* you what *The Trophy Effect* is about, or I'd have simply explained it in the first few chapters (and by now you'd be "smarter"). Instead, it's my intention that you experience it so profoundly that you never forget it. Therefore, I'm unwilling for you to step into your Trophy Room until it's time; until there's a reason to.

Frankly, the only way to extract all of the value you deserve out of observing *The Trophy Effect* is by collecting one insight at a time, which is how it's played out thus far, and why we've taken pause once more.

However, we are down to just one last honest conversation...

Note: As this process unfolds, you will be prompted to record your insights in either a journal or on a notepad. Although you are welcome to simply make mental note of your observations, it is highly recommended that you capture everything in writing, as suggested. To support you in this regard, a custom journal / workbook is available for download (free of charge), at www.thetrophyeffect.com.

Chapter 5 - *Looking for Proof*

Be honest. Are you truly able to accept how the fear of not being good enough has impacted your life? Or, are you one of those who believe that you either popped out of the womb unscathed or that you've somehow managed to outgrow it? If so, I urge you to finally surrender to the possibility that you are affected by this fear – as nothing can be overcome without first acknowledging its presence.

Indeed, we all know of people who have achieved success in spite of this fear. Many of us possess tremendous talent, have earned numerous degrees, or have accumulated great wealth. No one can deny that human beings are capable of doing some very amazing things.

Yet, if you are willing to reflect upon it, you will notice that one of the primary forces behind doing these great things is to *prove* to both ourselves and others that we are good enough!!!

Certainly, there are those who take effective action simply because they are living from an intention to do so and are determined to make a difference. But, even those of us who have mastered the ability to live *intentionally* still harbor the fear of not being good enough deep within our psyche – and somehow understand that our greatness has been achieved *in spite of* this fear and not because it doesn't exist. Thus, if we were being totally honest, we'd acknowledge that much of our life has been spent proving that we are good enough.

And why do we feel the need to *prove* that we are good enough? Because we are afraid that we are *not.*

Now, unless you've been living under a rock or really have been reading with your eyes closed, you're aware that I've been pointing at this premise since the very beginning. Yet, if this is true, then shouldn't you be able to look into your recent past and recall a time when you actually felt like this? Shouldn't you be able to remember specific instances when you were either frustrated with yourself for not following through or were otherwise present to your concern of not being good enough?

Of course you should – and very shortly you will be identifying at least one of those instances, which will then serve as your ticket into the Trophy Room!

And what is this ticket good for?

What is about to be revealed is the very secret behind the *Daisy Chain Dilemma*, thereby leaving you fully empowered to break this chain whenever you choose. You will also discover both *how* and *why* you've been more inclined to feel discouraged rather than inspired – which will leave you equally empowered to choose *inspired* at will. And finally, you will know with absolute certainty that you forever own the deciding vote on every tug-of-war between *survival* and *intention* – at which point, which force do you think you are going to align with most often?

As you can imagine, this process has impacted those who have embraced it quite profoundly. Yet this impact is more often realized over the course of several days or weeks, as one's "previous reality" is transformed and replaced with a higher level of awareness. Therefore, it's possible that you may not feel entirely different immediately upon the completion of our journey. However, I assure you that you *will* be different and that your "power of choice" will become increasingly evident over time…

Finally, I suggest that you allow yourself to be *moved* by what you're about to observe. Please be open to seeing the truth. Remember, your mind does not want you to see any of this. It will perceive it as a threat. Therefore, I suggest that you not even invite your mind to this party. Instead, come as your*Self.*

Now that our "pre-flight" checklist is complete, let's proceed with a few important questions…

If, in fact, the mind has access to proof that you are both *not good enough* and *a quitter* (which it has as a by-product of the *Daisy Chain Dilemma*), then every time you set out to accomplish something, wouldn't it be natural for the mind to question whether you are the right man or woman for the job? Wouldn't it have reason to doubt both your abilities and your willingness to stay the course? ***Thus, wouldn't the mind be justified in considering you a threat to your own survival?***

Go on. You can say it. Obviously, the answer is *yes*. And how often do you suppose the mind is faced with this concern? That's right; *every time* you set your sights on an outcome – and especially when you begin to move toward it. At which point, the mind evaluates the likelihood of you succeeding and weighs that against the risk that you could fall short (thereby exposing you to losing, looking foolish, etc.), which it would perceive as a threat to your survival. Then, after taking into consideration who you are *(not good enough to succeed)* and your history with regard to such things *(a quitter),* it determines how best to survive you through the situation and advises you accordingly. And, in light of the mind's concern that you are neither good enough *nor* likely to stay the course, what do you suppose that advice might be?

So, how does the mind make these evaluations? Where does it look to determine the nature of an impending threat and how to survive us through it? As was alluded to previously, whenever the mind perceives a threat, it looks into your *past* in search of any incident where you survived a similar threat (which, of course, you did, given that you're still here). For instance, situations where you may have been embarrassed, looked foolish, felt dominated, were wrong, made a mistake, fell short, or simply gave up – yet *survived* the incident either in spite of, or as a result of, any of these things.

In any such situation – once your mind has perceived it to be a threat and begins to search of your past for input on how to best survive you through it, it is looking for either one of two things:

1) **Proof that you're not good enough**; thereby confirming its suspicion that you are a threat to your own survival. Once it finds this proof, its surest option may be to have you *give up* right away. In other words, to take the *quick and easy* way out – which it can accomplish by having you quit, disassociate, act confused, pretend to get a phone call, go to the bathroom, etc. Again, if the mind finds immediate proof that you're not good enough, it could simply advise you to give up and be done with it, thereby surviving you through the threat rather quickly.

2) **Similar incidents where you felt similarly threatened**, yet did take some form of action and then ultimately survived. If you contemplate this option, you will notice that this would include any similar situation where you took any kind of action – because whether or not you were satisfied with the outcome – *you still survived!!*

Okay, let's suppose that you're a mind and you perceive a threat. How quickly must you be able to spring into action? In a heartbeat, right? And knowing that you're going to have to sift through a fairly large collection of incidents from the past every time you detect a threat, wouldn't you want those incidents pre-sorted and filed in an organized manner?

For instance, if you were perceiving a threat on the level of, say, a little discomfort having to do with stepping in front of a small group of people to deliver a speech, would you want your mind to react in the same way it did when you stepped in front of the class to read a poem when you were six? Come on now, you may have wet your pants back then – and that's probably not the first response you want your mind to offer up when it goes searching through your past.

If you're a mind who's faced with a threat and in urgent need of a survival response, you can't afford to spend time sorting through some disorganized collection of incidents when the pressure is on! Therefore, when would it make the most sense to evaluate and organize these incidents?

Well, if you were in need of a specific book at the library, would you be okay with waiting while the librarian sorted through a large pile of miscellaneous books or would you prefer that they be better organized before you arrived? Similarly, if you're a mind and the only reason you're even storing incidents is because you may need to reference them later, wouldn't it be wise to evaluate, rate, and organize those incidents *before* you put them into storage?

Of course it would – and since your mind is very wise, that's precisely what it does.

As it pertains to situations in your past where an incident caused you to associate to your fear of not being good enough – can you see that some of these situations were more intense than others, thereby causing you a greater level of anxiety or concern? In other words, can you see that there were times when making a minor mistake may have simply left you annoyed with yourself (thereby serving as little more than a *reminder* that you weren't good enough), versus other times when you may have suffered a more significant setback or felt even worse – which not only served as a reminder, but actually showed up in those moments as proof that you weren't good enough?

By simply looking into your own experience, you'll notice that because of your fear of not being good enough, your mind never overlooks any of these situations. In fact, it has mastered evaluating and classifying them in order to determine which ones to dismiss as "reminders" and which ones to hold onto as "proof." What's more, you will find that this all plays out subconsciously and within milliseconds, which means that unless you know to look for it, you're not going to observe it happening – which is why you never caught it happening before!

Now, with regard to how the mind rates these incidents (which is a process we'll soon be observing first hand), let's suppose that it performs its evaluation on a scale of "1 to 10," and has somehow decided to disregard those incidents that it rates at "3" or less, thereby suggesting that it must be classifying those incidents it rates at

"4" or more as proof, or as "keepers." Sort of like a fisherman who keeps all the big fish and throws back the tiny ones. Likewise, your mind is continually "fishing for keepers."

So, if and when the mind finds these "keepers" (which happens almost every time it perceives a threat), what does it do with them? That's right. It *keeps* them. And where does the mind keep all of "the keepers" it has perceived as threats and is retaining in support of the Daisy Chain? Where does it store all of the evidence that you're not good enough, and a quitter, and a threat to your own survival? And where, after separating the *reminders* from the *proof*, does the mind store every bit of this for future reference?

In the Trophy Room of course.

So, now you know. Yet, knowing what's in the Trophy Room is only part of the story, as the real value comes from knowing *what* goes on in this room and *how* it happens – both of which you're about to discover for yourself.

Remember, I promised you that we wouldn't enter your Trophy Room until it was time to do so; until there was a reason to. Surely, I could simply tell to you what goes on in there (in fact, I already have to some degree, as you now know that this is where your mind stores all of your "incidents" and all of its *proof*).

However, in order to fully appreciate what happens on the other side of this door, it is critical that you not step into the Trophy Room until the exact same moment as *the mind* itself – at which point, you'll be able to observe what it does while it's doing it. In other words, you'll be able to catch it *in the act*...

Chapter 6 - *A Just Reward*

So, how are we going to catch your mind "in the act?" How are you going to observe *The Trophy Effect* in action?

Simple. By throwing your mind *an incident* and watching what happens next. You are about to observe your mind evaluate and rate an incident and then store it as proof. You are poised to witness first hand how the mind does its job – including how it cherishes and then safeguards that proof. At which point, you'll pretty much be observing your *ego* in all its glory.

Of course, in order for this to happen, we must first identify an incident – which is your cue to begin searching your memory for one, as we're about to "toss" your mind one of your *own* incidents. To which end, please think back over the last few days or so with the intention of recalling a circumstance where you may have given up or stopped short. A situation where you failed to follow through and, as a result, clearly remember thinking that you weren't good enough (or otherwise recall feeling unworthy, incompetent, or disappointed by your inability to make something happen).

Again, the outcome is to recall an incident where you may have made a mistake or appeared foolish; a situation where you failed to live up to your own expectations or may have let others down as well. A moment when you specifically recall having a thought such as "what a dummy," or "what a loser" – or otherwise remember questioning your own self-worth. Once you identify at least one moment in your recent past when you recall feeling like this, please make note of this incident in your journal.

Do you have an incident?

If not, please do not read any further until you do.

* * * * * * * * * * * * * * * * * * *

Coaching: As you attempt to identify your incident, please know that you will soon be learning how to remain positive and intentional in the face of any such memories; meaning that any negative emotions that may arise during this process will soon be displaced by feelings of freedom and joy...

* * * * * * * * * * * * * * * * * * *

Remember; our mission is to observe your mind as it takes your incident and runs with it, which will require that you follow my lead as I walk you through this exercise. Obviously, I'll not be able to comment on what you are thinking or experiencing, so instead, I'll be describing for you the experiences of one of my many clients who participated in this process (and who has graciously permitted me to share his story). As you read of his experience, please allow yourself to be influenced and inspired by his responses to my questions and prompts, as well as his insights and breakthroughs.

As we move through this process together, I request that you allow yourself to stand both in his shoes and yours – *as one* – in order to *see what he saw* and *feel what he felt.* Once you do, I'm confident that you will come to realize that what you are observing is an actual representation of the functionality of your own mind as it processes your incident. If so, you will never forget what you are about to experience. You will always know the truth.

Therefore, let us begin. You and I, and *Jason...*

One of the most remarkable processes I ever conducted was with "Jason," a long-time client living in Manhattan, who originally came to me complaining of his inability to follow through on simple tasks. Jason is an amazing man, who had built a very profitable business for himself. What's more, he was extremely intelligent, full of life, and was proud to have paid for not only his mother's heart surgery, but for weddings for two of his brothers. Still, he always felt that no matter how well he was doing, he should be doing better – thus, he was often very stressed and rarely felt as happy or as fulfilled as he could be. In fact, in spite of his success, he confided that procrastination was only one of several undesirable "habits," which he felt contributed to his lack of self-confidence. Consequently, even as a graduate of New York University, Jason often felt as though, somehow, he just wasn't enough.

You see, Jason had no way of knowing that he was "living in a fishbowl" and that his concern was *innate* rather than *personal*, although he was certain that his concern was personal because he had proof. For even though his life was otherwise very full, he honestly felt that something as insignificant as his inability to complete and turn in his monthly expense report on time was evidence that he was personally defective. It was such a simple task, yet he struggled with it time–and–time again. So, for Jason, this issue definitely showed up for him *as proof* that he wasn't good enough – which is why we chose an incident related to this situation as his ticket into The Trophy Room.

Again, as I continue to describe how this process unfolded for Jason, please allow yourself to identify with your own incident (i.e., your own concern that you're not good enough) and follow along as an observer of his insights and revelations as well as your own…

At this point, my instructions to Jason were to visualize a specific moment in time when he was frustrated by his inability to complete his expense report. As it turned out, this had occurred several times the previous day, when he had initially promised himself that he would finish his report before noon. Then, after failing to do so, he had re-promised himself that he would complete it by 2 pm, followed by yet another promise for 4 pm – until he eventually ended up in bed without completing his report. As a result, he recalled feeling utterly incompetent (prompting a concern that he wasn't good enough) *every time* he failed to follow through, which caused him to realize that he had linked all of these incidents together. Even so, I instructed him to identify and focus on one specific incident.

In situations such as this, it's important to recognize that it doesn't really matter *why* Jason failed to complete his expense report on time. Whether he got distracted by something more important, received an urgent phone call, or simply chose to play video games instead – he *still* fell short. Remember, the mind is forever on the lookout for proof that you're not good enough – not for reasons to doubt itself. Therefore, as far as his mind was concerned, Jason's inability to submit his expense report in a timely manner was precisely the kind of proof it was looking for.

Now, with regard to your incident, please attempt to identify the specific moment within that incident when you recall thinking or feeling that you weren't good enough. Once you recall this feeling and what it was related to, please make note of it in your journal so that we can begin to figure out whether your incident is *worthy...*

Having advised Jason of our need to make this same determination, I asked him to recall and acknowledge that when his incident occurred, did he, *in that moment,* truly consider his inability to complete his expense report "strong" enough to serve as proof that he wasn't good enough or did it simply serve as a *reminder* (after all, it wasn't as if he crashed his Porsche into a telephone pole). In response, he assured me that he could clearly recall feeling that he wasn't good enough, thus he considered it *proof* – which meant that this incident was definitely *a keeper.*

In support of this same outcome, I request that you make a similar evaluation; for in order to gain access to your Trophy Room, you must be satisfied that you've identified an incident which clearly proves that you're not good enough. If you determine that your incident is simply a reminder and *not* proof, then please "toss it back" and recall another incident. Once you're satisfied that your incident is *a keeper,* you're good to go. Yet, just to confirm, let's review...

At this point in the process, Jason had qualified his incident as *a keeper.* And now *you* have likewise identified your incident and are similarly satisfied, correct? In other words, you have recalled an incident that represents a specific moment in time when you made a split-second decision about being a threat to your own survival; a moment when you came face-to-face with your fear of not being good enough and gave into it. A moment when the Daisy Chain had you hooked and you got reeled in. An incident where you doubted yourself so much that you're satisfied it's a "keeper." Right?

Well, in that case, my friend, you're in! You've got your incident – your *keeper* – which will finally enable you to experience *The Trophy Effect* in action. You have earned your ticket into the Trophy Room!

However, before we pass through this door with your "incident" in hand, I must pose one final question: What, exactly, do you suppose you are carrying into this room with you? What is it that you are about to put "into storage" forever? What is this "thing" that will be forever accessible to the mind as proof that you're not good enough? A ticket? A proof? A keeper?

I suggest not.

No. The mind needs *more.* After all, what you have in your possession is nothing less than the validation of your mind's greatest fear; something that it will display proudly as evidence that you've fallen short once more and are a threat to your own survival. You are about to enter this room with something that will provide lasting proof that your mind did its job – of a moment in time when you proved it right! What you have earned is a valued keepsake that your mind will treasure forever. Thus, what you are carrying with you into this room is your "just reward" for a job well done!

And what type of reward does one store in a Trophy Room?

You guessed it, a ***trophy***.

Notes -

Chapter 7 - *Knocking on the Door*

Do me a favor. Take a look at your trophy and tell me what it says.

It's blank, right? In which case, once we're inside the Trophy Room, how are you going to know where to put it?

Right now, the only thing we know for sure is that you awarded yourself this trophy in recognition of *not being good enough*; yet wouldn't that be true of every other trophy in this room (after all, isn't this the only reason they're in there)? Therefore, what do you suppose must happen before you make your way inside?

That's right. You must somehow "mentally engrave" your trophy in support of storing it in its proper place. And although you may not know for sure where it belongs until you step through this door, what we *do* know is that you're not about to toss it aimlessly inside and be done with it.

Frankly, there's no way of knowing how many other trophies we are about to find in this room, but even if this was the very first one, I'm sure you'd agree that you still need to ensure that it's "clearly marked" for future reference.

As promised, we're about to watch your mind "evaluate and rate" your incident – *a.k.a. your blank trophy*. Which prompts the question, just who is this "mind" that must perform this little task? Right again – it's *you!* Just like it's always been you. However, unlike all those other times, this time you will be fully conscious of the fact that you are doing it!

"What is necessary to change a person is to change his awareness of himself."

-Abraham Maslow

Consciousness is power! In actuality, you have been evaluating, rating, and storing these incidents in your Trophy Room your entire life. Furthermore, you are a veteran of innumerable tugs-of-war between survival and intention and have been sharing your fishbowl with *the fear that you are not good enough* ever since you were a minnow. Not to mention the fact that you've been caught up in *The Daisy Chain* since before you could read! The only difference between *then* (before you read this book) and now, is that *now* you know it!! Now you are aware.

And, once you walk through this door and discover "the secret" of *The Trophy Effect,* you may actually believe you know it *all.* Of course, as is true with any newly-acquired knowledge, how it ultimately impacts you is totally dependent upon what you *do* with it. However, since it's unlikely that you will ever forget what you're about to observe, you will *always* know what to do...

Hopefully, in the wake of what has been revealed to this point, you're already seeing things in a different (and more encouraging) light. By stepping into the Trophy Room, you will gain access to the final "light switch" of our journey, thus the opportunity to shed even more light on the prospect of living free of self-doubt and negativity. You are only moments away from discovering the source of that "little voice" that questions your every intention; thereby leaving you fully empowered to finally break free!

Are you ready to flip that switch? Of course you are. Yet before you do, there's one last task at hand – which means that you won't be going anywhere or won't be discovering anything until you evaluate and rate your trophy...

Cutting right to the quick, all that you need to know about your trophy is how you earned it and how certain you are that this incident serves as proof that you're not good enough.

First of all, did you award yourself this trophy for making a bad decision? Did you earn it for being victimized or abused? Was it for losing something? Did you get fired? Were you dumped by a lover? Or, did you earn it for something more routine – such as procrastination or for making a simple mistake?

In any case, assuming that you know how you earned it, the next step is to determine to what degree - *on a scale of 1 to 10* - you feel this incident *proves* that you're not good enough. As you recall, back when you initially perceived this threat (which was the source of the incident for which you were awarded this trophy in the first place), you conducted a similar subconscious evaluation – at which time you felt this incident deserved at least a "4 out of 10" or you wouldn't have retained it as proof.

With this in mind, please reflect back on this incident once more, only this time recall the specific moment when you remember feeling inadequate or thinking that you weren't good enough and notice how you felt at *that* instant. Go back and "feel" the proof. When you have a sense of it, please rate that feeling (again, from 1 to 10) and record it in your journal.

As for Jason, he was so frustrated by his inability to complete his expense reports on time, that when I explained this process and asked him to rate his incident, his response was both immediate and certain: "*15,*" he declared, "maybe higher." As you can tell by his assessment, Jason was not only thinking "outside the box" (the "1 to 10" box) but wanted to impress upon me (and now you) that this was no small issue for him. In light of this example, if you now feel that your incident deserves a higher rating, then by all means, please scribble through what you wrote and re-tell yourself the truth.

On the other hand, if you wonder how anyone could assign procrastination such a lofty rating, it's because there's no such thing as a *universal rating system* tied to *The Trophy Effect*. And although the mind may not actually rate each incident numerically, there's no question that some form of hierarchical evaluation is being conducted, which enables each trophy to be stored in proximity to similarly-rated incidents within your memory. As for whether or not your rating system equates with anyone else's, who can know? Each of us sees things in our own way, so we rate them as we see them. Therefore, if Jason felt that his incident was deserving of a "15," then that's how it showed up for *him.* Again, with respect to your own evaluation, you should go with whatever feels right for *you...*

Remember, our outcome is to replicate as closely as possible the manner in which your mind actually conducts this evaluation and rating process, including how it determines where to store your trophies and anything else that happens along the way. How this all plays out is at the very heart of *The Trophy Effect*, which is why I've taken so much time to explain each sub-dynamic, reveal every distinction, and inspire as many insights as possible. And although this process may appear fairly complex, from the minds perspective, all of this is nothing more than "business as usual."

In fact, the only thing *unusual* is the tremendous speed at which this dynamic occurs. For although we may be taking what seems like forever to dissect this process, the mind actually perceives a threat, evaluates and rates it, does it's thing in the Trophy Room, and advises you accordingly *all within seconds!*

Of course, the ensuing process of acting (*re*-acting, actually) on the mind's advice in the wake of any perceived threat (i.e., your immediate reaction, including whatever you say or do and then whatever you or others do in response to that) often prompts a chain-reaction that may last for hours or even days. However, this is an aspect of *The Trophy Effect* that we'll be addressing later, as our primary mission is to discover *what* it is and *why* it has so much control over your thinking. Which is precisely what we're about to do...

Now that you understand how and why you've been awarded this trophy and are fully associated to your incident, we are finally prepared to step into your Trophy Room – that specific "memory vault" which *The Trophy Effect* calls home. This is its domain. This is where it wields its power and has been doing so forever without you even knowing it! At least until now.

Again, our intention is to replicate how this dynamic plays out as accurately as possible so that you can understand and appreciate the functionality of your own mind. And although we're slowing the process down considerably, be reminded that what you're about to observe all takes place within a matter of seconds...

Last minute check list!

You:

* *have your trophy*

* *are clear how you earned it and how you rated it*

* *are clear that you're about to put it into storage for future reference*

* *are equally clear that, in real time, you would have perceived this threat and been awarded this trophy only moments ago*

* *understand that what you are about to do consciously is something that you've been doing unconsciously forever*

* *wonder what might possibly occur in this room that could have so much power over your thinking*

* *wish I would just shut up and let you go in already!*

You got it? Then in we go…

And please allow me to get the door…

"For one who has conquered the mind, the mind is the best of friends. But for one who had failed to do so, his very mind will be his greatest enemy."

–Bhagavad Gita

Notes -

Chapter 8 - Burdened by Proof

As we finally step into your Trophy Room, please know that you may or may not be able to perceive everything there is to "see" all at once. However, if you surrender as fully as possible into the metaphor as this process unfolds, I promise that you will soon feel as though you are standing right in the middle of it…

After leading more clients than I can count through this exercise, I can assure you that every one of them reported experiencing exactly the same thing. However, there are certain details that typically show up as unique to each individual. As we move through this portion of the process, I'll be inviting you to observe specific things for yourself while describing how those same things showed up for Jason. Still, I suggest that it will play out more powerfully if you allow yourself to experience it exactly as it shows up for you.

In any case, your trophy's almost home – so, let's figure out where it belongs…

As for Jason, he had just stepped into his Trophy Room when he realized that what he was looking for was a *trophy case.* "Precisely," I assured him – for where else would one store a trophy? And how do you suppose Jason's mind responded to his realization that what he needed to find was a trophy case? That's right, it granted his wish – so, in no time at all, he found himself not only standing before one of the most magnificent trophy cases he'd ever seen, but was certain that his trophy belonged in that case…

And since your mind is equally-accommodating (not to mention the fact that this is its job), I invite you to notice that immediately upon our arrival, you, as was Jason, have been magically deposited directly in front of a similarly magnificent trophy case. Not just any case, mind you, but the trophy case in which you're about to store your trophy!

Amazing, isn't it? But of course it is! After all, your mind has performed this little task countless times. Thus, after it evaluates and rates your incident, it charges directly through your Trophy Room door – with trophy in hand – and knows exactly where it's going. And that's precisely what happened this time, which is why you're standing exactly where you should be.

However, at this point, the mind does pause to catch its breath – and to ponder – as we're about to observe…

Meanwhile, there stood Jason, directly in front of his trophy case, prepared to place his trophy inside. Just as you should now be imagining yourself standing in the exact same position, similarly prepared to receive the very same instruction that I gave him, which is: *Please open the trophy case...*

Okay, that's your cue! And as you visualize yourself reaching for the door handle, please pay particularly close attention to what you observe in response to my following question: What do you see inside this case immediately upon opening the door? In fact, what *must* you see?

Please take a moment to make note in your journal of what you see…

If you're not certain, please stay with the metaphor and acknowledge what you suspect you'd see had you just opened a trophy case you've visited countless times before for the exact <u>same</u> purpose (which, of course, was to put trophies in it). But if you're still not sure, let's check in with Jason to discover what he observed…

"No doubt about it," Jason confirmed as he opened the door and looked inside, "what I see are trophies. *Lots* of other trophies."

Bingo! Lots of trophies. You see, we've all been here before. Yet, it's important that you see this for yourself – so do you? Have you opened your trophy case and discovered that there are, indeed, lots of other trophies already in there?

Again, being fully aware of how and why you awarded yourself this trophy, your mind has instinctively steered you toward this specific trophy case – so whether you earned it for being victimized or abused or were simply reprimanded by your boss for being late to a meeting – your mind knew precisely where it was going. Therefore, no matter how you earned your way inside, are you able to see that there are other trophies already in this room that you earned for either doing or enduring something similar in the past?

At this point in the process, I asked Jason this same question, to which he replied "of course!" – reminding me that he had actually awarded himself several trophies the previous day for not completing his expense report on time. In fact, he soon came to realize that he had accumulated an entire case full of trophies over the previous few weeks for procrastination alone!!

In the wake of this realization, Jason was *on a roll.* He could clearly see that he had been awarding himself trophies for just about everything that he had ever done "wrong" and that all of them were in this room! Within no time, he had surrendered fully into the metaphor and found himself standing squarely in the middle of his Trophy Room; visualizing trophies and trophy cases all over the place!

Still, as telling as this may have been for Jason, let's check back in with you – as you may not be experiencing everything quite as effortlessly as was he…

In fact, you've yet to accomplish what you came here to do – and since your mind would have surely added your trophy to its collection as soon as it stepped into this room, what are *you* waiting for? Oh, that's right – *me* – as I confess to drawing out this most recent series of events in order to demonstrate that there's no way to enter your Trophy Room without noticing the trophies that are *already* in there.

In recognition of which, it's critical that you see that this isn't the first time you've been in this room or the first time you've put a trophy in this case…

Meanwhile, having already come to this conclusion on his own, Jason was still on a roll and quick to admit that he could tell at a glance how he had earned each and every trophy in his trophy case. And although every one of them had been awarded as proof that he wasn't good enough, he was none-the-less enthused and inspired by his ability to follow the metaphor so effortlessly.

Again, Jason was not only able to visualize every trophy he had earned the day before, but most of the ones he'd earned within the last few weeks – and could even recall feeling that he wasn't good enough every time he earned one!

However, as he came to realize the extent to which his life had been diminished by everything he had just observed, Jason was no longer as enthused or inspired as he had been...

"What a *loser*," he sighed, as it all began to sink in. "Michael," he pleaded, "you must help me with this procrastination! *So many trophies!* I feel as though there's no way out. Just look at all this proof of my inability to take control of my life!"

By this time, it was evident that Jason was no longer impressed by his ability to visualize everything so easily – as he was noticeably annoyed and embarrassed. For what had begun as the simple task of placing a single trophy into a single trophy case had suddenly snowballed into him standing face-to-face with several weeks' worth of proof that he wasn't good enough…

"Unbelievable," he muttered, "where does it all end?"

And yet, as Jason was about to discover, there was no end in sight. For what had been revealed was little more than the tip of the metaphorical iceberg. In fact, it was becoming painfully clear that his Trophy Room was home to dozens of additional trophy cases. And within those cases was stored even more evidence of his futility with regard to circumstances such as squandered business opportunities, his reluctance to playing full out (or not following through), failed relationships (or the fear of even initiating one) and, as insignificant as it might otherwise seem, the fact that he was routinely late for appointments – *among countless others!*

"This is *very* depressing," he lamented, as the agony of it all continued to sink in…

And, as it was sinking in, I knew that it was time to "pop the question" – and so I did… "Jason," I wondered, "just how big is this Trophy Room of yours?"

"Michael," he confessed, "it's the size of *a gymnasium.* And I've been filling it with trophies since I was very, very young…"

Notes -

Chapter 9 - *The Revelation*

So, what about you?

Have you been able to visualize anything at all with regard to *your* trophy room? Are you willing to admit that you've been "filling it with trophies since you were very, very young?"

Depending upon whether you were simply entertained by my account of what Jason discovered in his Trophy Room or actually took it upon yourself to "play along," you may or may not know the answers to these questions.

If not, that's fine – for as you may have surmised, I'm about to walk you through this metaphor – one step at a time – so that you may experience it with the same intensity and clarity as did Jason. Yet, as we re-trace his footsteps, I suggest that you allow yourself to be influenced by the essence of what Jason experienced rather than by the specific nature of his room or its content.

If you are willing to acknowledge what's so, you will soon be envisioning yourself gazing upon your very own collection of trophies within your very own Trophy Room. And yet, there's no way to predict how many trophies you'll find or the size of your room until you step fully into the metaphor and visualize it for yourself.

For instance, although Jason's room held dozens of trophy cases for procrastination, you may not even have an issue with procrastination. In fact, you may discover that you have fewer than a dozen cases altogether – yet that remains to be seen…

As for how large your Trophy Room may be, I've had participants visualize rooms as expansive as warehouses or "about the size of an attic." Some clients have envisioned their Trophy Rooms to be the size of museums, storerooms, or hallways – while others have simply described it dimensionally, such as "20 x 40."

In any case, it's important that you discover your own truth – to which end I suggest that you allow yourself to visualize your Trophy Room "as it shows up," rather than attempt to "imagine" its size in advance.

Right now, the only thing we know for sure is that you've had little more than a glimpse of *The Trophy Effect*. Why? Because you cannot possibly comprehend it completely until you've experienced everything that happens inside your Trophy Room and until I reveal several additional distinctions having to do with your relationship to what's in there.

Of course, you may have already been able to visualize your room to some degree – yet even if you have, I urge you to remain open to what lies ahead; allowing yourself to envision an even clearer image of your room and its content as we continue with our journey...

As you'll recall, prior to us observing how this process played out for Jason, you had just discovered "lots of trophies" inside your trophy case and were about to add another to the collection. Therefore, please allow your-self to slip back into the metaphor and imagine that you are standing in front of your trophy case once more…

Given that your mission is to determine where within this case you should store your trophy, can you see that the best way to figure that out would be to simply "read through" the trophies that are already in there? Then, once you identify those which most closely match the one in your hand, *you're in!* Therefore, please visualize yourself reading as we continue…

As you begin to envision what is "engraved" on each trophy – thereby recalling not only how each trophy was earned, but its rating as well – what must you be reminded of as you read them? In fact, what are you actually *forced* to reflect upon as you read each existing trophy in an attempt to figure out where to put your new one?

You got it. ***A whole lot of evidence that you're not good enough!*** Shelf-upon-shelf of proof that you are not only a threat to your own survival, but obviously have been for quite some time. Trophies-upon-trophies, representing similar incidents that could have occurred years and years ago or as recently as today. Either way, they're *all* in here.

Or, it could be that you've earned so many similar trophies that you've filled more than one case (just as Jason's room held several cases for procrastination). For instance, if your incident had to do with being late, how many times in your life have you been late? If you earned this trophy for being forgetful, how many times have you forgotten something (or don't you remember)? Or, perhaps you didn't stick to a diet or otherwise failed to lose some weight you wanted to lose. In which case, how many trophies have you earned for this issue over the course of your life?

On the other hand, it is possible that you awarded yourself this trophy for something that hasn't happened very often, which means that you could be standing before the only case of its kind in your entire Trophy Room. However, if you are clear that you earned this trophy for something that seems to keep happening over and over again, then there's a pretty good chance that you've filled more than one case with similar trophies.

Still, whether or not you find more than one case filled with trophies similar to the one you brought in here, these are but a few of the countless others you'll likely discover once you begin to contemplate everything else in this room. In fact, now would be the perfect time to imagine yourself "stepping back" from the trophy case you've been focusing on in order to visualize *all* that there is to see…

Accordingly, I invite you to do just that – and to let it *sink in.* Allow yourself to recall how many other times in your life – and for how many other types of incidents – you have awarded yourself trophies for not being good enough…

Maybe you've never been too good at relationships or at socializing in general. How are you at spelling, or at sports, or at holding your own when discussing world events? Were you ever neglected or abused or otherwise disrespected? Have you ever failed to accomplish an objective – or simply failed to try – yet awarded yourself a trophy either way? In any case – and whether or not any of these particular examples ring true – are you willing to see that you have, in fact, been awarding yourself trophies for various other types of incidents?

Assuming that you see this – thereby confirming that the trophy in your hand is *not* the only one you've ever awarded yourself for not being good enough – about how many trophy cases would you say are in here?

No matter how many you think you "see," are you at least beginning to get "a feel" for the size of your room? Or, how about the size of the impact on your psychology?

As you are able to appreciate its size, are you also beginning to feel the *pain?* After all, you simply stepped into this room to make a quick deposit, and the next thing you know, you're browsing the shelves at "*Trophies -R- Us*" feeling like an incompetent loser! Of course you feel the pain; a nagging, mystifying pain that you've known to "come and go" forever – yet have never been able to explain...

Frankly, how could anyone *not* feel the pain? How could you or anyone else spend any time at all in the presence of this much proof of anything without being convinced that it was true? In fact, after contemplating only a few of the countless trophies in this room – yet having done so within the shadow of them all – how could anyone remain enthusiastic about their prospects of accomplishing anything or not be concerned about being good enough to hold onto whatever they already have? Well, more often than not, "they" can't, which is a primary source of what most of us have come to know as *resignation.*

In light of all this, I welcome you to one of life's best-hidden and most agonizing dichotomies. The fact that no matter where you go, *your Trophy Room goes too!*

Anytime you set your sights on something worth-while (establish a goal) or acquire something of value (achieve a goal), you cannot help but feel some degree of fear. Naturally, this fear prompts the concern that you're not good enough – which causes your mind to slip into survival – which leads it (you) directly into your Trophy Room. Where, of course, you are treated to an exhibition of anything and everything that ever caused you pain. It's akin to having a personal traveling "museum of horrors" where *you* are not only the curator and the ticket seller, but your own best customer!

In a nutshell, here's what there is to get: whenever you are contemplating a meaningful course of action and are about to make a decision, there's no way of doing so without being negatively influenced by all the trophies in your Trophy Room – which is where your mind delivers you whenever you're concerned that you're not good enough – which naturally occurs every time you are about to take action or are faced with an important decision. Hence, ***all* of your meaningful decisions are made in the shadow of your trophies!**

In other words, no matter what you set out to accomplish, your fear of not being good enough causes you to doubt yourself – at which point, you are subconsciously transported into your Trophy Room – where you can't help but notice all the evidence of your futility (which justifies your fear). At that moment (although you can easily get "sucked in" for hours), for no less than a few brief excruciating seconds, you are forced to deliberate a room full of proof that you will likely fail – which causes you to either re-think your outcome, not take an action you were about to take, or give up completely!

And this, my friend, is the primary premise of *The Trophy Effect!*

Do you get it? Was it worth it? Or is this revelation showing up a lot like other things in your life – not quite what you anticipated? Not quite good enough…

Well, if you're not overly impressed, I suggest that it may be for one of two reasons: the first being that all you know of *The Trophy Effect* thus far is that it causes you to focus on your failures (which naturally diminishes your confidence and your passion), and the second being that I've yet to reveal *how* we're going to turn all of this around. Which we *will.* However, you should be prepared for things to get a little bit worse before they get better, as we're about to delve even deeper into the most painful aspects of this dynamic in order for you to understand the power it has over your psychology. Even so, I assure you that there is a light at the end of our metaphorical tunnel – so please hang in there…

In order to "delve deeper," I ask that you focus on your Trophy Room once more, only this time describe it as best you can in your journal – visualizing its length and width and even "the lighting" – or anything else you may happen to notice.

Once you've made note of these features, I ask that you begin to "browse around" in search of some of your more predominant trophies – such as any you may have earned for being abused, for losing a job, or for being rejected by a lover. Have you ever been fired or downsized? Have you ever invested in something foolish or been conned? Have you ever been cheated on or had a lover leave you for someone else? Have you ever had a serious disease? You see, among the many issues or challenges that could possibly occur in one's life, these types of incidents tend to show up as "the biggies." Thus, they're likely to have earned you some very large trophies! Which is why you shouldn't have any trouble recalling them if you have them – and pretty much *everyone* does...

Fortunately, incidents such as these do not occur too often (at least not for most of us). Yet, when they do, they're likely to have a devastating effect on one's psychology. Why? Because we not only award ourselves *giant size* trophies, but in the wake of these events, we tend to earn even more trophies for associated "sub-incidents," which generally occur within days or weeks of the "big one." As a result, we are inclined to recall an entire series of events whenever we're reminded of *the biggies* – which, themselves, are typically displayed in a manner that renders them virtually impossible not to notice.

In any case, thanks to *The Trophy Effect*, each of us is reminded of these "significant incidents" every time we *re*-visit the Trophy Room. For instance, suppose you intend to wake up early to exercise but over-sleep instead. *Bingo!* You not only miss out on an invigorating workout, but earn yourself both a brand new trophy and a ticket into the Trophy Room for another glimpse of your *biggies.* Or, how about when you finish off an entire quart of ice cream when you're supposed to be on a diet? You got it – both another new trophy and a trip into your Trophy Room for an "encore showing" of the big ones. And, as it pertained to not completing his expense reports on time, Jason later realized that many of his "biggies" were awarded in recognition of earning so many individual trophies for procrastination in a single day!

Again, no matter how you earn your way back into your Trophy Room, there's no way of doing so without being reminded of your giant-sized trophies every time you do. And yet, most of us tend to wonder why we can't seem to forget about these things…

Well-meaning friends and relatives implore you to simply "let them go." And yet you can't. And I suggest that "you can't" for two specific reasons:

1) Your mind is actually retaining all of these incidents for *future reference* (in support of your survival, which I will better explain very soon), and -

2) How can you? How can you forget any of your trophies – let alone "the biggies" – when you're in here as often as you are?

Surely, the best way *to let go* would be to stay out of your Trophy Room altogether, yet that isn't likely to happen unless you overcome your fear of not being good enough. Of course, this isn't likely to happen either unless you give up being human (you do recall the part about this being an "innate" fear, don't you?) Or, you could simply choose not to award yourself a trophy when this fear shows up – but this doesn't appear to be something that you've been willing or able to do.

Otherwise, all that you can do in response to this well-intended advice is *roll your eyes,* for both of us know that the only thing you've ever been able to let go of is *the advice* – not the incidents. For thanks to *The Trophy Effect*, you haven't been able to steer clear of your Trophy Room long enough to avoid being reminded of them. At least, not *yet.*

So, exactly how much pain do you suppose you've endured as a result of this dynamic? Are you able to see how being consistently reminded that you aren't good enough has taken its toll? Can you now see why you are often less-than-enthused to embrace new opportunities? Why there are days when you just can't seem to get going? Perhaps days when you don't even feel like getting out of bed? Times when you've caught yourself being a lot more willing to give up than inspired to go for it? Finally, can you see how *The Trophy Effect* has diminished your passion by overshadowing it with a room full of proof that passion only gets you in trouble? If so, how does all of this make you *feel?*

Assuming that you're not feeling too good, you should be able to appreciate how these feelings can quickly snowball into something even worse: that "two-headed monster" born of resignation and self-doubt that tends to show up even when things are going well…

You achieved a goal or succeeded at attaining something and yet it isn't quite enough. There always seems to be "a string attached." An asterisk. A caveat. Are you able to see how almost every celebration is dampened by the concern that something isn't quite right or that something might still go wrong? A fear that "the other shoe may drop" or that it could all go to pieces tomorrow?

For instance, you finally got that new job or the big promotion, yet how long will it be before "they" find out that you aren't really qualified or that *they* otherwise made a mistake?

Or how about when you finally mustered the courage to invite someone out and they agreed? Although you achieved your initial outcome, you then had to prove that you were worthy of their company - which is no small concern given your fear of not being good enough. So, instead of feeling empowered and joyful, you felt anxious and were reduced to *hoping* that it would all work out. Or, perhaps, you chose to have a couple of cocktails to overcome your anxiety. After all, sitting across from someone while wondering if they think you're good enough will have that effect on you.

Finally, please reflect back upon all the times you were excited about the prospects of attaining something but then decided not to go for it when confronted by a circumstance that caused you to "re-think" your capabilities. Have you ever thought about starting a business or following a passion – or maybe even did so – but then failed to follow through in the face of such a concern? And how many times have you simply "changed your mind?"

What's important to consider in the wake of incidents such as these is that there is no way to give up on *anything* without "taking a hit" to your psychology. You see, from the mind's perspective, it doesn't matter *why* you gave up – or even if it made perfect sense to do so – *you still quit.*

At which point, the "Daisy Chain" kicked in – and as it did, yet another page of proof was added to that *tear-jerker* of a novel your mind has been composing ever since you "quit" for the very first time - *"the story of your life."*

Of course, none of this would weigh on you as heavily as it does if you simply kept this subconscious "collection of failures" on the shelf. However, both of us know that you've been referring to it at just about every turn; especially when considering your options or contemplating what to do next.

In any case, having lived your entire life in the shadow of the *Daisy Chain,* you have probably already survived many of the scenarios described in the last few paragraphs.

Given which – and in light of what you now know about *The Trophy Effect* – is it any wonder that you are rarely as happy as you could be? In fact, how could anyone be happy after spending time in *your* Trophy Room?

And yet, no matter how poorly you may feel on occasion, there are other times when you're feeling pretty good. Times when things are going really well or when you feel like you're on a roll. And although we all know of people who appear to be *un*happy a lot more often than not (and now you know why), there are others who seem to be fairly well adjusted and happy most of the time. So what's up with that? Do they not have a Trophy Room?

No, that's certainly not it. Yet there is a simple answer as to why some of us experience more joy than others or seem to be happy for no particular reason – and why some of us are able to *roll with the punches* while others often feel like they *just got punched.* In other words, an answer to the question that everyone has been asking since the beginning of time.

And that answer awaits you across the hall…

"Happiness depends on ourselves."

–Aristotle

Chapter 10 - *The Other Side of the Hall*

So, what is the secret to being happy? And how can any of us ever really be happy with this *Trophy Effect* thing going on?

Well, before I answer that question, let's check back in with Jason. Who, after contemplating everything in his gymnasium-size Trophy Room, was feeling pretty *low*...

"Michael," he lamented, "no wonder I so often feel like my life is weighing me down. Please promise me that there's some way out of this mess."

"Of course there is," I assured him, "as you will soon come to discover by way of your *other* Trophy Room..."

As you are aware, Jason was both an educated man and someone who had proven himself in many ways – and although he admitted to being overwhelmed by all of his newly-discovered "bad" trophies, he was happy to have not only paid for his mother's heart surgery but for weddings for two of his brothers. And, when counting his graduation from NYU among his several blessings, there were many things for which he was truly grateful. However, although there may have been times when he reflected upon these things more fondly, *this* certainly wasn't one of them…

"So, Jason," I exclaimed, with the intention of snapping him out of his melancholy state, "now that we've taken our little tour of your "bad" Trophy Room, are you ready to leave all of this *doom and gloom* behind?"

"Please," he pleaded, "tell me about this *other* Trophy Room…"

To Jason's delight, I was prepared to do even better than that – for by "stepping across the hall" he would soon be able to explore it for *himself*. Which is exactly what you and I are about to do as well, just as soon as you visualize yourself putting your *bad* trophy in its case where it belongs. Which, I encourage you to do right now before you become so depressed that you won't feel like going anywhere...

Therefore, out we go – back through that same worn door and into the hallway in search of your other Trophy Room. As I mentioned, it's just down the hall, so you can't miss it. In fact, do you remember that *little man* behind the curtain? Well, your other trophy room is located *behind* that curtain, which means that we're going to have to deal with him once more. Yet, this time, I promise that we'll be able to walk right past him...

However, before I make good on this promise, please allow me to finish telling you about Jason and what I shared with him as we set out in search of his other trophy room. The "Good" Trophy Room...

That's right. The *Good* Trophy Room! For where else do you suppose you've been storing your "good" trophies?

After all, don't you do "good things"? And don't good things happen to you? Absolutely! And even though our deepest fear is that we're not good enough, each and every one of us has done lots of wonderful things. And shouldn't you be acknowledged for the wonderful things you do?

Of course you should! And, in fact, you are actually going to have to recall one of those "wonderful things" fairly soon, as we're about to meet up with that little man behind the curtain – and he's not about to let you into your Good Trophy Room without a *good* trophy – which is why he wouldn't let us in the *last* time.

You see, just as you had to identify a worthy incident from your past as your ticket into your Bad Trophy Room, you're going to have to do the same across the hall in order to get past "the guard" (that little man)...

So, what have you got? Have you achieved any significant outcomes? Have you done anything especially worthy? Or, are you simply in need of a better explanation as to how to earn a *good trophy* in the first place?

As I shared with Jason, the way in which you and I earn good trophies is essentially the same as how we earn the bad ones. We establish outcomes or have expectations and, as life plays out, we either do good things or good things tend to happen – for which we sometimes award ourselves good trophies and sometimes we *don't.*

In other words, just as there is across the hall, there's a "rating system." And because your mind only awards good trophies for incidents it considers *worthy*, you are not going to find any trophies in your Good Trophy Room that were put in there "by accident." Nor are you likely to observe your mind passing out good trophies like candy, as the evaluation process on this side of the hall is far more selective than it is in the other room.

What's more, not only are the entry requirements more restrictive, but having already had the "pleasure" of meeting your door guard, you know very well what he's going to say if you should show up *without* something worthy. Of course, it's not like you retain everything on the other side of the hall either, so no matter how stringent your "personal rating system" may be, there's always the possibility that it's serving you just fine…

In any case, we're about to observe how Jason's rating system served him, for as he and I approached the "little man" guarding his Good Trophy Room, we took pause to consider a few of the *qualifying incidents* from his past. Again, this was a man who had recently saved his mother's life, had blessed two of his siblings with magnificent weddings, and had graduated third in his class from NYU!

Even so, I asked Jason to be brutally honest about how he had rated these incidents at the time they occurred. For it was critical that we determine whether or not he had actually awarded himself good trophies for these incidents *when they happened* – before we attempted to enter his Good Trophy Room.

You see, being entirely truthful about one's "personal rating system" is vital with respect to how we finally turn *The Trophy Effect* around – which was not only true for Jason, but is equally true for you, as we're about to explore your truth as well.

Therefore, just as we were careful to honestly assess the size and content of your other room, it is every bit as important for us to paint an equally-accurate picture of your *Good* Trophy Room.

With this in mind, I reminded Jason that our outcome was to identify any trophies that he had awarded himself *back then* (at the moment when the "good thing" occurred), as opposed to awarding them now – in retrospect – for things he had previously considered nothing more than *nice* memories.

Remember, this is not a memory vault – it's a *Trophy Room.* If we were searching for "happy memories," we'd have sought out that room (as you'll recall, we passed it by in Chapter Four), which is where you've been keeping track of all the "pleasant things" that have happened in your life. However, these are incidents that have been stored so deep within that vault that you think about them only on the rarest of occasions – such as at reunions, or at weddings, or when reminiscing with old friends.

In any case, we're not looking for "happy memories," we're looking for *proof.* Proof that you are good enough. Proof that you are *worthy!*

Given which, this is precisely what we'll be searching for as we begin to explore your Good Trophy Room, where the only way to have earned your way inside is with a good trophy. As you've come to learn, your mind has been awarding you *bad* trophies at just about every turn, which has caused you to spend an inordinate amount of time in your Bad Trophy Room, feeling *pain.* Now we're about to discover how much time you've been spending in your Good Trophy Room – feeling *happy.*

Again, it is not our intent to re-evaluate anything from a fresh perspective, but to ascertain precisely how you rated your incident at the moment it occurred. In other words, did you or did you not award yourself a trophy and store it in your Good Trophy Room at that time? And it's important that we make this assessment *before* we step into this room for two reasons:

1) So that we are not distracted or influenced by what's already in there, and -
2) To identify one of your "award-winning" incidents in order to show the associated trophy to the door guard so that he'll let us into the damn room!!!

After all, you saw how he reacted the last time when we showed up without one.

At this point, having emphasized several times that we were not looking for happy memories, I asked Jason to think back on the day of his mother's surgery. And although he must have known that he was doing a "good thing," did he ***truly*** appreciate and acknowledge himself sufficiently *in that moment* to award himself a trophy for it? In other words – and in keeping with the metaphor – did he or did he not award himself a good trophy for paying for his mothers operation?

"Not at all," he admitted. "I can see that I did not. It was as you suggested – I knew it was a good thing, but I certainly didn't expect any *special* recognition."

"Jason," I exclaimed. "You're telling me that you paid for your mother's surgery yet didn't consider it worthy of any "special recognition?" You filled up dozens of trophy cases in your other room with bad trophies that you earned for not completing your expense reports on time, but didn't feel that saving your mother's life was deserving of a single *good* trophy?"

"That's right," he confessed. "I've never looked at it like this, but you asked me to be honest – and I can clearly see that we are *not* going to find a trophy in my Good Trophy Room for having paid for my mother's operation…"

Sound familiar? And although you may have never funded a relative's surgery, can you recall a time when you *did* do something especially magnanimous yet *didn't* consider it worthy of a trophy? I'm speaking metaphorically, of course, as there would have been no reason for you to award yourself trophies before reading this book. Which is why I ask that you contemplate your response to the following question from outside the context of this metaphor: Isn't it true that you've done lots of great things for which you failed to award yourself good trophies?

If so, then perhaps you and Jason share a similar reasoning…

"So, Jason," I was compelled to ask, "how can that be?"

"She's my mother," he explained. "I had the money – there was *never* a question."

Very noble and very selfless. I told you that Jason was an amazing man. And I suspect that you share a similar inclination as well. After all, you and I were "taught" that being *humble* is an important thing; that we shouldn't be one "to blow our own horn."

However, with regard to your general sense of happiness and fulfillment, if you fail to acknowledge (and routinely reflect upon) all of your worthy deeds and accomplishments, it's doubtful that you will ever feel exceptionally good about yourself. In which case, you're probably not going to have to worry about "being humble" very often…

Still – and with all due respect for "being humble" – I would suggest that all any of us ever wanted to do was to contribute and make a difference. You and I <u>are</u> "the gift." Yet, if we do not consider ourselves worthy, then we will not be empowered to give "it" away. And, if we do not feel good enough to share the gift of our wellbeing, then what, exactly, might we share with others? The gift of our unworthiness? The gift of our frustration? The gift of our moodiness? Oh boy! Where do I get in line for some of *that?*

On the other hand, no one is interested in receiving a gift from someone who is less than sincere, nor in receiving the "gift" of anyone's *ego.* Yet, it is my intention that you come to realize that withholding good trophies from yourself has never been, nor ever will be, in your best interest! In light of which, I urge you to remain open to observing what has been true for you with respect to awarding yourself good trophies *in the past* and how it will serve you to evaluate things far less critically *in the future.*

"Humility does not mean that you think less of yourself, it means that you think of yourself less."

-Ken Blanchard

Appreciating Jason's expression of humility, I then asked him about the weddings…

"Nope," he assured me. "No trophies. Like I said, I knew I did good. People came up to me all evening and thanked me for a wonderful time. I shrugged it off. As I told you, I had the money. There was never a question."

Once again, very noble. And please be certain that I'm not knocking nobility. I'm not at all suggesting that you should give up humility for arrogance or trade in your willingness to do things anonymously for the need to be bathed in glory. Neither am I interested in you becoming vain or self-absorbed.

In fact, it's my intention that you discover your ability to *transcend your ego* altogether as you come to experience your Self as more fully empowered, worthy, and happy. All of which is possible because you and I have every ability to acknowledge our magnificence on a regular basis while still remaining humble, grateful, and giving. It's just that most of us do not believe that we have this ability. Most of us do not think that we can have it *both* ways – and, as Henry Ford suggested; "whether you think you can or think you can't, *you're right.*"

You see, in addition to our primary concern of "not being good enough," our fishbowls are home to a secondary consideration known as "either / or." For this reason, human beings are inclined to believe that in order to achieve one thing, we must give up another – or at least sacrifice a part of something in order to deserve a piece of something else.

Sadly, this belief is prevalent within the culture (S*ocial Conditioning,* if you will) and plays a key role in preventing us from living as powerfully as we otherwise could; often limiting our experience of freedom and abundance (for instance, how many times have you been told that you "can't have your cake and eat it too?"). It's also why we tend to feel that we can't possibly "pat ourselves on the back" *and* remain humble at the same time.

It's also the primary reason Jason failed to award himself a trophy for saving his mother's life or for supporting his siblings in such an unselfish manner – as well as a contributing factor to why he responded as he did when I finally asked about his graduation…

"So Jason," I continued. "Please tell me about earning your degree. Did you by any chance award yourself a good trophy for graduating from such a prestigious university?"

"As a matter of fact," he replied, after pausing for a moment to contemplate his response, *"I did!* I can see that I gave myself a trophy on the very day of my graduation!"

Well, how about that? After four years of intense study, Jason had actually awarded himself a *good* trophy – which was not only well deserved at the time, but would now allow us to get past his door guard and into the Good Trophy Room to scope out the "rest of his collection."

First, however, there was one more thing I needed to know... "Jason," I asked, "what was the rating you assigned to this trophy you earned for graduating from NYU?"

"Three," he was quick to acknowledge, "I gave myself a *3*."

"For graduating *third* in your class?", I presumed.

"Perhaps," he replied. "You see, although I was happy – okay, *somewhat* happy – I had worked very hard to be number one! So, in that regard, I came up short."

"Of course," I agreed. "And what happens when one "comes up short?" What happens when one has proven to themselves that they aren't good enough to accomplish what they set out to do? More to the point, what did *you* do?"

"Oh my," Jason realized. "I did just that. I gave myself a *bad* trophy! And because I truly wanted to graduate at the top of my class, I can see that I gave myself a bad trophy every time my grades were less than I had strived for…"

Yes, indeed – Jason had awarded himself bad trophies for falling short. And although he had earned only a single good trophy (with a measly "3" rating) over the course of his four years at NYU, he had managed to accumulate a significant quantity of bad trophies over that same period of time.

Thus, on the very day that Jason accepted his diploma from a major university – a day that should have been filled with joy and celebration – the best he could feel was "somewhat happy."

And what kind of ratings did Jason assign to all the trophies he earned for falling short?

"Tens," he acknowledged. "Without a doubt – *all tens.*"

So, there you have it. And even though you may have never awarded yourself a bad trophy for failing to graduate first in your class, can you recall any similar situations where, although you accomplished a relatively major objective, you may have fallen short on some level? Perhaps a time when you either finished first or outperformed nearly everyone else, yet still felt that you could have done better? And although you may have actually granted yourself a *good* trophy for whatever you did accomplish, you also awarded yourself a *bad* trophy for falling short – or several bad trophies for incremental failures along the way?

Again, can you see how we are not necessarily set up to win? Can you see how *The Trophy Effect* is still affecting you over here across the hall? Still, I promised you that we would turn all of this negativity around – which is precisely what we will begin to do just as soon as we step into *your* Good Trophy Room. First, however, allow me to reveal what Jason discovered when he finally stepped into *his*...

As you can imagine, Jason wasn't exactly thrilled to learn that his *good* trophy came with so many *bad* trophies attached. However, I was able to console him by suggesting that he would likely feel better once we began to explore his Good Trophy Room. At which point, with the expectation that we would soon be admiring the rest of his "greatest hits," we flashed his graduation trophy at the little man standing guard (who, as I recall, rolled his eyes when he spotted the "3") and darted though the door -

And with that – as Jason was both surprised to discover and quick to announce – it was *dark*.

"Well then," I began, in advance of suggesting the obvious, "hit the light switch."

"There is no light switch," he replied. "Only this lousy light bulb, dangling on a cord from the ceiling" – which, being fully aligned with the metaphor, Jason had been equally quick to visualize and was just as quick to "turn on" by pulling the little chain…

In so doing – although he had no way of knowing – Jason had not only saved us from stumbling around in the dark, but had also shed light upon the second premise of *The Trophy Effect*. A premise no less significant than the first (which, as you recall, was the fact that your Bad Trophy Room is filled with a lifetime full of proof that you're not good enough and that you make all of your important decisions in the shadow of that proof) – yet one that offers up considerably more promise than it does pain. As you shall see, just as soon as we acknowledge what Jason saw…

"So, Jason," I asked in the glow of his dimly lit trophy room, "what do you see?"

"Well," he replied, "not much. Are you sure we didn't step into a broom closet by mistake?"

"Why," I wondered, "do you see brooms?"

"No. But I don't see very many trophies either – and this certainly *isn't* a gymnasium."

"Hmmm," I thought – for although he had only begun to make sense of what he was "seeing," I could tell that Jason wasn't overly impressed with either the size or the content of his Good Trophy Room…

"Not quite as spacious as that "auditorium" across the hall?" I quipped – just prior to assuring him that there was no reason for dismay, as each of us is born with the ability to expand our good room at will. Still, I was interested in learning about any good trophies he may have observed, as *that* would be very telling…

"Jason," I continued, with all the empathy I could muster, "since both of us know that you neglected to acknowledge yourself for saving your mother's life, I would hope that you weren't expecting to find any trophies in here for having washed your car or for paying your bills on time. Still, it's entirely possible that you have awarded yourself good trophies for other things – in which case, I ask that you 'take a look around' and tell me if you see any…"

However, rather than offer up a specific account of what he did or didn't see, Jason was suddenly struck speechless – remaining that way for several moments – until finally breaking his silence by announcing an *epiphany!* He had *seen the light* – and it wasn't the one hanging from the ceiling. In fact, he had been moved so profoundly that he could hardly contain himself – although, at first, he was pretty much unable to say anything at all…

Even so, it was obvious that Jason had been "transformed," when he finally shared that what he had experienced was both *devastating* and *magnificent!* That he was both *saddened* and *empowered.* And, above all, he was very, very *grateful…*

What Jason revealed was that the source of his gratefulness was a level of understanding that he had never been present to before. For as terrible as he felt about everything in his bad room, he felt even worse about *the absence of trophies* in his good room. In fact, what Jason had come to realize was that there was only one reason why his Good Trophy Room wasn't any larger or any fuller than it was; a reason that not even he could deny…

In that moment, Jason knew that it had always been up to *him.* He could see that it was he who had not been awarding himself good trophies and, as a result, he had been settling for "somewhat happy" rather than joyful.

He had chosen humility over passion – which, he realized, was nothing more than *false* humility at that – having been born of his *ego* and not of his soul. And, in the shadow of everything he had just observed, it was becoming painfully clear that the "emptiness in his trophy room" was merely a reflection of something he had been feeling deep inside; *an emptiness in his heart…*

Yet, in the wake of these realizations, Jason was immediately heartened by the sense that he was *already* blessed with the ability to turn everything around!! That because it was *he* who had chosen not to award good trophies in the past, it was *he* who had the power to do so from that moment on – thus, the power to <u>choose</u> to be happy!!!

Again, what Jason had stumbled upon was the <u>second</u> premise of *The Trophy Effect* – which is that our socially-conditioned inclination to remain humble and reserved in the face of our accomplishments both governs and impedes our ability to extract as much joy as there is to be had from those accomplishments.

In essence, what Jason realized was that it was he, and he alone, who had been living with his finger on the "mute button" and that it was he who had decided that *toned-down* was the appropriate, responsible, and expected way to live one's life.

At least until *now...*

"Your playing small doesn't serve the world.
There's nothing enlightened about shrinking so that
other people won't feel insecure around you...
We are all meant to shine, as children do."

-Marianne Williamson

Notes -

Chapter 11 - *Off to See the Wizard*

As you can imagine, in the wake of his epiphany, Jason was once again "on a roll." However, should things not be unfolding for you at a similar pace or if you have yet to experience a similar breakthrough, I encourage you to remain fully engaged until you *know in your heart* that you are no longer willing to settle for "somewhat happy." To which end, I invite you to not only embrace what Jason shared about his good trophy room, but allow it to inspire you.

On the other hand, given what you now know about the mind, can you see how it would be inclined to dismiss the majority of Jason's observations and insights? In light of which – and in consideration of the fact that you've obviously read this far – I commend *you* for having not given in to any compulsion you may have felt to put this book down. After all, from your mind's point-of-view, just about everything you've learned thus far could be perceived as a threat to your survival.

You see, the mind is perfectly satisfied with the notion of "either / or" and it has no issue at all with the limited content of your Good Trophy Room. Consequently, your mind will resist any attempt to alter the "status quo" and is likely to equate any influx of good trophies with an expanded sense of "Self" – and I'm sure you can appreciate how it feels about that. For wouldn't you be upset with the prospect of your tug-of-war opponent growing stronger?

* * * * * * * * * * * * * * * * * * *

<u>Coaching</u>: *If you are truly committed to a breakthrough and intend to extract as much value as possible from this process, you must remain fully intentional from this point forward. For the mind is not only a formidable opponent, it is also <u>very</u> sneaky...*

* * * * * * * * * * * * * * * * * * *

In fact, I can pretty much guarantee that your mind will prompt you to dismiss this process as baseless or as nothing more than "pop-psychology." Or, it may "trick" you into believing that you have no problem with awarding yourself good trophies or with spending time in your Good Trophy Room. And, I can assure you that it will do its best to talk you out of capturing your responses in writing or completing the Exercises. And, although your mind is clearly the source of all this confusion, it will have you believe that *you* are the one thinking these thoughts and that you are simply being "practical."

And yet, as is validated by the fact that you're still here, the intentional "you" (the Self) has stayed the course. Why? Well, I suggest that it's because something about this metaphor "strikes a chord." It hits home.

Something at the very heart of this process speaks to that part of you that has somehow known this all along. That part of you that has always felt as though you were suppressing something magnificent deep within yourself and wondered how and when you would finally break free.

Well, "that part of you" can finally stop wondering, because the opportunity to acknowledge and embrace your inherent magnificence is now at hand – as the next step toward unleashing your true Self is the one that we are about to take into your Good Trophy Room. Which means that after having spent the better part of the last ten chapters focusing on fear and survival, we are about to contemplate something a lot more *empowering...*

With this in mind, please think back over the course of your life and recall an exceptionally positive experience for which you are certain that you would have awarded yourself a good trophy. Again, the outcome is to identify an incident that you would have considered worthy of a trophy *the moment it occurred* (as opposed to re-evaluating or upgrading any "happy memories"). Therefore, please keep this in mind as you ponder your past and then make note of this special occasion in your journal…

Have you identified an incident? If so, how'd you rate it? As you know, Jason believed that his graduation from NYU warranted no more than a "3," yet that still earned him a ticket into his trophy room. In light of which, I suggest that you not get too hung up on the rating, as we'll be "tweaking" your evaluation criteria fairly soon anyway. What's more important is that you've recalled the truth about a worthy incident from your past and you are now imagining yourself holding the associated trophy in your hand.

As you visualize this trophy, it is crucial that you allow yourself to be present to this truth for several reasons, the most critical having to do with your capacity to be transformed by it once you experience it. However, our first priority is to make our way into your trophy room so that such a transformation can occur…

Therefore, and without further adieu, please "hold your trophy high" as you envision yourself stepping up to the curtain that stands between you and this room - -

"Halt! Who goes there?!" cried the little man standing watch at the door. "Who goes before "the Great and Powerful Wizard of the Trophy Room?"

Wizard of the Trophy Room? You gotta be kidding! Talk about a lack of humility! And although it would seem that his *only* job is to make sure that you've got a trophy before letting you into your trophy room, he's acting like he owns the place! Of course, since this is typical of how the little guy reacts *whenever* you show up, it would appear that, somehow, *you've* created a monster…

In fact, over the course of the next few chapters, you will not only come to discover *how* your door guard got turned into a monster, but the truth about *your* role as "Dr. Frankenstein." But for now, there's a Good Trophy Room to be explored, so kindly flash the good "wizard" here that trophy of yours and follow me…

As we step inside, please be reminded of my recommendation to allow yourself to be inspired by Jason's experience without being unduly influenced by it. In other words, please enter with an open mind. For all we know, what's awaiting you on the other side of this door *is* a gymnasium rather than a broom closet (although that is highly unlikely), but please take care to assess both its size and its content as accurately as possible.

You see, no matter how large or small you determine this room to be – nor how many good trophies you do or do not see – what is about to be revealed is nothing other than a representation of your *past*, not your future!

So, with all this in mind, please allow me to get the door…

Well, what do you "see"? Should we find a light switch? Or are the lights already on? In any event, rather than attempting to determine the exact size of this room at once, I suggest that first you "take a look around" with the intention of recalling and identifying some of your especially large trophies (the "biggies"), as those are likely to inspire further insight...

Therefore, please allow yourself to slip back into a reflective state of consciousness (or whatever it takes for you to recall a few of your most precious memories). Think back upon a time when you felt truly happy or appreciated to the degree that you would have awarded yourself a good trophy and are now able to visualize that trophy here in this room. Remember, we're not here to upgrade any happy memories, but are instead looking for incidents that you considered worthy the moment they occurred. Incidents that *proved* you were good enough.

Yes, that's the ticket! Proof that you were good enough! Specific situations where you recall feeling certain that you were good enough in the eyes of someone you considered important enough for that to matter; such as your father, or your mother, or a teacher, or a boss. In consideration of which, do you see any trophies in this room that you earned for proving your worthiness to any of these people? If so, please make note of them in your journal…

Whether or not you've identified any trophies that you earned for being good enough for any of these "important individuals," are you willing to acknowledge that *this* has been a primary consideration when awarding yourself trophies in the other room as well? Can you see that you have, in fact, been awarding yourself *bad* trophies for feeling less than worthy in the eyes of certain people you didn't want to disappoint?

If so, how many bad trophies have you earned over the years for letting any of these important people down? Have you ever wondered whether you were good enough for your mother or your father (or for whomever it was that cared for you as your mother or your father)? Have you ever awarded yourself a bad trophy for not measuring up to a sibling or a peer? Have you ever felt less than worthy in your own eyes?

Of course, it could be that none of this applies to you. However, if the shoe does fit, please allow yourself to wear it – as this *theme of disappointment* tends to play a key role in how we evaluate incidents on either side of the hallway. And why is it that we so often feel this way? Because of the *Daisy Chain,* of course…

On the other hand, how many trophies do you see in your good room that represent situations where you *did* make any of these important people happy or proud? How often were you acknowledged by any of these individuals for a job well done or otherwise felt as though you met with their approval? Be honest, and then make note of any such incidents in your journal.

Finally, how many *other* good trophies do you see in this room?

How about situations where you exceeded expectations? Have you ever finished first or otherwise excelled? How about times when you overcame a challenge or were recognized by your peers?

What about simply having fun? Any dream vacations or other adventures which were so magnificent that you awarded yourself a trophy for simply having the intelligence to make them happen? How about great sex? Those times when you gave fully of your-self or received love from another; times where you felt passion and were fully alive. Surely, there are at least a few tro-hies in here for moments like these… Yes? *No?*

Still, remember the rules! For no matter how many of these "nice" memories you may be stirring up, you mustn't forget that we're hunting for *trophies*, not memories. Why? Because our out-come is to determine how often you've actually spent time in this room putting good trophies away. How often have you provided yourself with the opportunity to bask in the joy of it all? How often were you in here not only adding to your collection, but "drinking in" all of the evidence of your magnificence?

How often have you been *forced* to reflect upon how lucky you are and what a privilege it is to be living *your* life? How often are you in here feeling empowered and grateful?

Well, if you're like most human beings (and are willing to admit it) you've likely discovered that it's *not* very often at all. Still, we all know of people who appear to be earning good trophies on a fairly consistent basis. People who are obviously spending a lot more time in their good trophy rooms than not, which has left them feeling a lot more care*free* than care*ful.* People for whom life tends to show up as effortless and fun and who share their wellbeing and their love openly and freely – which then sets into motion a sort of *positive* Daisy Chain that results in even *more* trips into their Good Trophy Room…

Pop Quiz! Having observed that spending time in your *Bad* Trophy Room robs you of your passion, what might happen if you spent more time in your *Good* Trophy Room?

a) It would allow you to *bask in the joy* of all your good trophies.

b) It would inspire you to feel worthy, empowered, grateful, and happy.

c) Both "a" and "b" – so why not hang out in here more often?

Unfortunately, although (c) may be the answer of choice, most people come to realize that their Good Trophy Room looks pretty much like Jason's. Meaning that most people can count on one hand the number of times they've visited this room over the course of the last few months or even years. Which means that they can also count on one hand the number of times that they've spent any amount of time in this room "taking it all in."

Now, in spite of this, do people with meager good trophy collections still do good things? Of course they do. Do people who fail to award themselves good trophies on a regular basis still lead productive lives? Without a doubt. Are those who spend very little time in their Good Trophy Room still able to rise to the top of their professions? Are they able to excel in business, be recognized for their achievements, or even have "good" sex? Absolutely.

Yet, do these individuals tend to extract as much enjoyment as possible out of everything they do? Do they routinely consider life a privilege and share their blessings with others? Are they set up to win the majority of the tugs-of-war between intention and survival? Are they inclined to take setbacks in stride or feel happy and fulfilled on a regular basis?

No. Not at all.

In light of which, if you have already come to observe how the Daisy Chain has *reeled you in* and are beginning to suspect that you *are* one of "these people" – then I encourage you to own up to it. For no matter how annoying this may be, the truth will ultimately set you free!

Free to live *intentionally* rather than *out of survival.*

In fact, I invite you to "own up to" and embrace all that you've learned about *The Trophy Effect* thus far – and to be willing to continue to do so from this point forward. For what is available on the other side of "owning up to the truth" is nothing less than the ability to exercise *full autonomy* over your own psychology.

Therefore, I encourage you be as truthful as possible with regard to assessing the content of your Good Trophy Room – for until you are able to acknowledge what you are up against, you will not be empowered to turn it around…

"To grow, you must be willing to let your present and future be totally unlike your past. Your history is not your destiny."

–Alan Cohen

Chapter 12 - *A Whole New Ballgame*

So, what's the verdict? Have you been able to make sense of what you discovered in your Good Trophy Room? Were you able to identify any "biggies" – and did they lead to the discovery of any other good trophies?

Before you respond, you may be interested to know that after identifying the one good trophy for graduating from NYU – and after a thorough examination of a life-time worth of memories – Jason ultimately called off the search of his "broom closet," declaring it an exercise in futility. Thus, when all was said and done, he ended up with a grand total of "one."

That's right, *one.* So, for those keeping score, it was something like this: Bad Trophy Room: 5000+ Good Trophy Room: 1. Of course, in actuality, there was no way for Jason to count all of his bad trophies, so the 5000+ was simply an estimate – but you get the picture. The Good Trophy Room never stood a chance. *And neither did Jason.*

So, what's your final score?

Frankly, many of those who participate in this process do discover more than one trophy in their Good Trophy Room, yet rarely is it more than a dozen or two – and more often than not, it's less than a handful (typically, just a few "biggies"). In fact, there have been quite a few participants who were unable to locate even a single trophy. In which case, if you're having trouble identifying more than a few, you're not alone.

Consequently, the vast majority of participants have acknowledged that their Good Trophy Room is significantly *smaller* than their Bad Trophy Room. In fact, I've heard of good rooms that were no larger than storage closets, offices, or pantries – with many containing nothing other than a single trophy chest.

On the other hand, I've had clients tell me about Good Trophy Rooms that contained dozens of good trophies. In light of which, if your search yielded a similarly large quantity of trophies, then you'll be that much further ahead of the game when we finally begin the process of expanding your good trophy collection – which we will be doing very soon.

In any case, it's important that you "call it as you see it," so please do…

Again, and in most cases, one's *bad* room is likely to dwarf ones *good* room – so if you're in this same boat, do not be disheartened. Remember, as Jason discovered, *awareness is power!* For once you acknowledge that you've been putting trophies in both rooms based upon evaluation criteria that you made up, you'll be poised to take back control!

Yet, before this can happen, it's imperative that you see this for yourself. What's more, it's important that you "up your intention" and remain especially resolute for the remainder of this chapter, for what is about to be revealed could easily trigger your mind to take evasive action. Therefore, please do not allow yourself to be dissuaded by anything it may whisper in your ear…

Here's a question for you: Why is it that some people have larger or smaller Good Trophy Rooms than others and why do some of us award ourselves more or less good trophies than others? What's up with that?

Well, it has everything to do with one's rating system *and the door guard...*

With regard to your rating system, how easy or difficult is it for you to earn your way into your Good Trophy Room? Do you find yourself in here several times a day? Several times per hour? Or, like most human beings, not very often at all? Are you in here whenever you lend someone a hand or make someone smile or only on those rare occasions, such as graduations or in the wake of some other major accomplishment?

If the latter rings more true for you, let's explore why that may be…

First of all, how do you suppose your rating system came to be? Do you think you were born with it? Do you remember being taught how to evaluate trophies by your parents? Did you learn how to rate trophies in Kindergarten?

No matter how it originated, who do you think created it? Who do you suppose determines whether or not you deserve a trophy for helping a little old lady across the street or whether they should be reserved for winning Olympic Gold? Who do you think decides whether an incident is worthy of a "3" or a "10"?

As I'm sure you've realized by now, the simple answer is "you." However, it's actually more of a *team effort,* that "team" being you and the door guard. However, since you're the one who trained the little guy (as I'll explain shortly) and are pretty much accountable for anything he says and does, you'd look pretty silly if you attempted to pin everything on *him.* Therefore, even though he's the one who pulls all the strings behind the scenes and is responsible for all of your subconscious considerations, it's still *you* – and always has been you – that's in command of the ship!

Consequently, it was you who invented the evaluation criteria by which you awarded yourself all of the trophies you discovered in your Good Trophy Room. Meaning, of course, that it was you who established the criteria by which you failed to award yourself trophies as well. Even so, what's also true is that you had no idea that any of this was happening until you read this book – so please do not award yourself any bad trophies for something you knew nothing about. However, now you *do* know – so from this point on, *it's a whole new ballgame!*

Of course, as is true with any new game, it's imperative that you understand "the rules" – which is why we are about to take a closer look at the "rulebook" that governs this entire process; the rulebook you employ for rating and awarding trophies. The rulebook you never knew to exist even though *you* wrote it. The rulebook you handed over to your door guard (the one you never knew to exist) the day you put him in charge of both trophy rooms – *which you never knew to exist either!*

Which tends to prompt the question; doesn't this make you wonder what else you may not know?

And yet, we can afford to put this question on hold for the moment, because in light of what you *do* know, you already have the power to transform everything! In fact, now that you've learned about survival, the Daisy Chain, both trophy rooms, and *The Trophy Effect,* we're on the very cusp of tying this entire process together. At which point, you'll able you to assume fuller control over all these factors – including the door guard! After all, you've always been his boss, you just didn't know it. But now that you do, you can finally put him to work for you rather than against you…

Speaking of the door guard – and knowing that he oversees both trophy rooms – why do you suppose he only stands watch over the *good* room? Have you noticed that you're able to store trophies in the *bad* room all day long without being hassled – yet whenever you show up at the Good Trophy Room door, he's all over you?

As you'll recall, when I initially walked you through this process, you earned your way into your good room with a trophy you had *borrowed* from this room rather than a new one. Therefore, you were never able to observe what the little guy does when you first show up at the door; which is to determine whether or not your incident is worthy of a trophy or if it's simply a nice memory. After which – more often than not – he sends you back down the hall to store that *nice memory* where it belongs. In other words, he is not only there to ensure that you don't get into your Good Trophy Room without a trophy, but he's actually in charge of determining whether your incident is deserving of a trophy *or not.* No wonder he acts like he owns the place!

In any case, how do you suppose he knows how to rate your incidents or which ones deserve or don't deserve trophies? Well, with regard to the *good* room, his evaluation guidelines are based entirely upon what serves *you!* Remember, you wrote the rule book. You set the standards. And although you may have done so subconsciously, you still made the call. You "learned" about happiness. You were taught how to be happy and when to be joyful by the culture and your personal environment.

Thus, how the mind awards good trophies is not driven so much by survival (as it is on the negative side), but is influenced by both your *beliefs* and your *intention* – and ultimately governed by your decisions. And, as you've learned, where do you make all of your important decisions? That's right, in the Bad Trophy Room.

You see, you long ago determined what it would take to please you – and, in response to a series of these subconscious decisions, established at what level you would allow yourself to experience a full measure of pleasure or joy. Which means, that it is always in alignment with these *previously established guidelines* that you determine whether or not something is "worthy of enshrinement into your sacred trophy room."

Thus is revealed the third premise of *The Trophy Effect,* which is the notion that good trophies are extremely *special* – and, as such, are extremely *rare.* For why else would you have established such restrictive entry requirements or hired a door guard?

Assuming that *your* Good Trophy Room is not overflowing with trophies, are you willing to accept that this is because you have "bought into" the *cultural notion* that happiness is attainable only as the result of some form of pursuit or special activity? And can you see how this belief then shapes your thinking with regard to whether a particular experience is deserving of a trophy or not?

What's more, if you and I really could be happy *at will* or if our most pleasurable emotions were too readily attainable, wouldn't that somehow render these experiences less valuable or less sacred?

Again, I'm suggesting that this manner of thinking arises from a "cultural notion" which implies that happiness and fulfillment are *outcomes* (that must be attained*)*, rather than *states of mind* (which are able to be expressed intentionally). Even the United States "Declaration of Independence" states that its citizens are entitled to the right to pursue happiness. Notice that it does not declare our right to be happy "just because we say so." Therefore, even though we are *entitled* to happiness, you and I must still *pursue* it – which would imply that happiness exists somewhere other than here and now.

As you contemplate this notion, are you open to seeing that it is the belief (hence, the *expectation)* that life's most pleasurable experiences are both sacred and scarce that renders them less attainable? If so, here's a question worth pondering: Do we assign fewer good trophies because we acknowledge fewer peak experiences – or could it be that we enjoy fewer peak experiences because we assign fewer good trophies?

Are you also willing to see that if happiness is something that must be "attained" then it must be uncommonly special? After all, who would want to pursue something that wasn't special or go out of their way to attain anything that wasn't worthy of the effort?

Along these same lines, would you be willing to acknowledge that you consider *passion* to be even more special – therefore something that you would expect to experience even less often? After all, if you were able to bring forth passion on a more regular basis, wouldn't that tend to minimize its significance? Wouldn't that tend to "water down the experience" and make it routine? And, as we all know, *passion* is anything but routine, right?

Given all this, are you beginning to understand your built-in resistance to awarding yourself good trophies? And, upon factoring in your previously-acknowledged aversion to appearing too full of yourself or otherwise less than humble, is there any question as to why your door guard isn't passing out good trophies like door prizes?

Of course not. Good trophies are special!

Therefore, unless you either do or experience something exceptionally worthy, your door guard will likely direct you back down the hall where your incident is destined to spend eternity as nothing more than a nice memory…

So, there you have it. A thorough explanation as to why your Bad Trophy Room is so full and why your Good Trophy Room is not - and an equally thorough explanation as to why most of us tend to feel only "somewhat happy" even on our best days.

Oh, and you also discovered that you hired and trained a door guard who thinks he's a Wizard and who acts like he owns the place.

So, what are you going to do about all this? Do you feel like you finally know enough to turn *The Trophy Effect* around? Or are you still in need of a little coaching?

And just who is this door guard anyway?

"Too many people undervalue what they are and overvalue what they are not."

-Malcolm Forbes

Notes -

Chapter 13 - *The Light at the End of the Tunnel*

With all due respect, how long are you going to allow your life to be run by some "little man behind a curtain?" How long before you sit your door guard down and put an end to all his *wizardry?* When are you going to let him know who's really in charge?

Remember, you trained this guy. He works for you. Yet, as the keeper of both trophy rooms, he's been a *pit bull* on the good side of the hallway while a *sieve* on the other. However, this is where you have the power to take back control because the process by which he evaluates and rates good incidents is only as selective as it is because of *you!* You wrote the rulebook and established the guidelines. Of course, you did so unwittingly and at a very early age – but how long are you going to live your life out of decisions you made when you were too young to know better?

In fact, you have every ability to spend as much time in the Good Trophy Room as you desire. After all, it's *your* trophy room. Who is ultimately in charge of your life? If you choose to award yourself a trophy for getting up on time or for brewing a great cup of coffee, who says you can't? If you feel that you deserve a trophy for working out or for clearing your emails, simply let the door guard know. In the end, it's *his* job to align with *your* beliefs and values – which means that once you consciously and intentionally choose to modify your evaluation criteria, your wish is his command!

Even so, the little guy isn't likely to embrace any such modifications unless he's convinced that it's "safe" to do so. Until then, he's certain to perceive any *shift in policy* as a threat to your survival and will resist even your strongest intention with all his might. Yet, why is your door guard so preoccupied with your survival? Well, his cover is blown – so I may as well come clean; standing watch over your trophy rooms is only his "part-time" job. For although he never strays too far from either room, you otherwise know this little fellow behind the curtain as – *your mind...*

Yes, it's true. This obnoxious little man with the very large ego is, in fact, your mind. He, whose sole purpose is survival. The one who would prefer that you simply "itsy-bitsy" yourself through the rest of your life and who prides himself on how well he's survived you thus far! As a matter of fact, in spite of whatever challenges you've had to endure, your little "wizard" has done his job each and every time! You survived them *all* – which is why he's not at all interested in you tampering with any of the rules or guidelines that have gotten you this far.

Indeed, your existing rules and guidelines have gotten you this far! And although they've rarely caused you to thrive, there's no question that they've enabled you to survive! Your little wizard has got it down! By playing off your fear of not being good enough, he's always known that if he can simply steer you clear of trouble and maintain the status quo, he'll be able to ensure your survival right up until "check out." By which time, you will have successfully tip-toed your way through an ordinary life, that may or may not have been sprinkled with moments of "somewhat happy" along the way. Of course, since happiness has nothing to do with survival, he'll still consider it a "win" provided that you make it through safely, which will have happened thanks to *him!*

However, you will be "tampering" with your existing rules and guidelines fairly soon, for how else are you going to create a future that is anything other than a regurgitated version of your past? How can you expect to evolve a more powerful psychology unless you spend significantly more time in your Good Trophy Room, or expect to break free of all the negativity unless you consciously steer clear of your Bad Trophy Room?

Ultimately, your "door guard" will be happy to enforce any new guidelines you establish. However, when you initially bring forth an intention to modify your evaluation criteria (in advance of awarding yourself more good trophies), I assure you that he will do all that he can to talk you out of it. Therefore, there's a very good chance that you will soon be engaged in one of the most critical tugs-of-war of your life...

Again, your mind has absolutely no problem with you playing less than full out. After all, if you were to cultivate more passion or confidence, you'd be tempted to dream grander dreams, which you would likely want to pursue – *which could result in failure!* For this reason, your mind is certain to perceive any increase in good trophies as a threat to your survival.

Therefore, you must be prepared to override your mind's "instinctual resistance to your personal growth" – as your door guard is bound to *dig in his heels* until he's convinced that any relaxed rules or guidelines are not going to expose you to a threat that might cause you to feel bad, look foolish, or otherwise appear inadequate (which, as you can imagine, would be just about any threat at all).

However, if you remain dedicated to this process by staying the course, your mind will eventually align with your "modified evaluation criteria" (while simultaneously establishing new neural-connections within your brain), at which point you will discover it to be just as vigilant as ever in support of ensuring the survival of your *new* point-of-view!

In fact, this is precisely how one builds "emotional muscle." This is how you grow! For once your door guard is convinced that you mean business, he will proudly stand guard over your new "way of being" (your new rules and guidelines) in support of the *Self.*

Yet, if you allow your mind to prevail, you are destined to discover why most people *don't* change. Why it is that when most of us attempt to modify any form of behavior, we ultimately throw in the towel – whether it's overcoming a fear, trying to lose weight, or attempting to break free of an addiction. For when the mind shifts into survival, it is doing what it was *designed* to do – which it does so powerfully that the *Self* loses out much more often than not. Therefore, as was pointed out in the second chapter, your mind will likely win almost every tug-of-war unless you remain dedicated to "living on purpose" – where awareness, intention, and courage take precedence over survival!

Still, it's critical that you not underestimate the power of the mind – which is because the very same instincts that ensure our survival are the ones that also deter us from staying the course.

For instance, in the case of habits or addictions, if an existing behavior provides so much comfort that kicking that habit may be perceived as a threat to your immediate well being, your mind will resist any attempt to modify that behavior. You see, your mind doesn't care if the addiction or habit could cost you a job or a relationship (or even cause health challenges down the road) as it is simply concerned with what is happening in the present and how to best survive you through *that.* At which point, it will compel you to choose a course of action that prevents you from losing, being dominated, being wrong, feeling bad, or appearing not good enough.

Even so, there is something rather curious about the manner in which this all plays out. For although your mind is prepared to award you bad trophies for incidents that prove you aren't good enough, it does so only <u>after</u> doing its best to steer you clear of any such incidents. After all, since feeling like you're not good enough is painful – and because the mind is wired to resist feeling pain – it is inclined to avoid the very situations it is searching for in order to award you trophies. And yet, once a trophy-worthy incident *does* occur – and you've earned one – it relishes the moment! Strange, isn't it?

You see, *paradox* is the playground of the mind and its favorite saying is "I told you so." The mind loves to predict the future based on what has occurred in the past – and considers it *a win* whenever it warns you that something could happen and then ends up being right about it (which is both the source of "self-fulfilling prophecy" and why it is so difficult to overcome addictions or depression). In fact, how many times have you caught yourself thinking: "I *knew* that was going to happen?"

However, now that you're aware of this dynamic, you'll be empowered to turn it around, as this particular mind function can just as readily be employed to your advantage. The key is in knowing that although *negative* thoughts and emotions beget more of the same, so do *positive* thoughts and emotions – which is a contributing factor to how the "Law of Attraction" works within the mind.

Remember, the mind loves to be right and to win. Thus, it will ultimately align with your desires and support you in achieving anything you *expect* to achieve! Of course, this also means that if you believe that you *are* a victim or are convinced that you *are* depressed (as opposed to simply *being* a victim or *being* depressed in the moment), the mind will predict more of the same and will persist in "being right" about that. After all, it told you so.

Yet, if "you" (*the Self*) are able to convince the mind that you intend to achieve a desired outcome and are willing to push through any fear or obstacle to do so, then it will be more than happy to award you good trophies for stepping beyond your fears rather than bad trophies for giving up. Hence, it will appreciate and embrace "being right" about you being an *achiever* rather than "being right" about you being a *quitter.*

Again, whether you think you *can* or think you *can't,* you're right! Therefore, it is critical that you demonstrate to the mind that you are aligned with your own intention by awarding yourself all the good trophies you deserve. Once you're actually doing so (you'll be learning how in Chapter Nineteen), you'll have begun to train your mind to "be right" about overcoming obstacles; thereby reconditioning it to say "I told you so" in appreciation of your accomplishments rather than in recognition of your failures.

Once this dynamic "kicks in," your mind will not only welcome new challenges, but will enjoy proving you right when you overcome them; prompting in a major shift of your *default mindset* from "reactionary" (avoiding fear or challenges) to "intentional" (embracing possibilities)! Given which, I encourage you to begin this practice even now, by bringing forth as much intention as possible for the remainder of our journey – as you are much more likely to be transformed if you participate *on purpose...*

"There is nothing either good or bad, but thinking makes it so."
– William Shakespeare

Chapter 14 - A Little Common Sense

By now, you've likely come to appreciate the degree to which you have allowed *fear and survival* to shape your thinking. And although such an appreciation is critical, the single most important thing that you can do in support of turning *The Trophy Effect* around is to fill your Good Trophy Room with as much evidence of your worthiness as possible!

Of course, while this is sure to make a difference on the positive side of the hallway, one can ill-afford to forget about that room full of "conflicting evidence" across the hall. After all, what good would it do to maximize the flow of *positive* energy from your Good Trophy Room if you were unable to mitigate the considerable *negative* influence of your Bad Trophy Room?

What is to keep any positive thoughts or emotions from being overwhelmed by the negative energy that is likely to emanate from your existing bad trophies or any you may be inclined to earn from now on? In fact, if the fear of not being good enough is innate, how is it possible to prevent this fear from "raining on your parade" of good trophies?

Indeed, the fear of not being good enough *is* innate – thus it isn't going anywhere, anytime soon. However, *you* are – as there is yet another room we are about to explore – and it is in this room that you will soon learn the answers to all these questions…

Therefore, please allow me to lead you "back down and across the hall" to a very special room we passed along the way. A room you probably didn't even notice – as most people don't – nor do they spend much time there even if they do. And yet, this is the *very* room we've been seeking all the while.

This is where you and I are about to make sense of – and *neutral-lize* – the Daisy Chain Dilemma. This is where we'll be turning *The Trophy Effect* around so that we can put it to work in your favor!

Best of all, given that your mind is significantly more interested in *survival* than it is with *higher consciousness*, this is the only room in your mind that's "off limits" to your door guard!

In light of which, I invite you to not only enjoy this little respite from your *ego* but to pay especially close attention to what you're about to observe inside – *as we're almost there...*

...Let's see, this first door reads... "Unfinished Projects" – nope, that's not it, and I trust that you won't be storing too much in here any longer... and this next one..."Broken Promises" – likewise, I'm sure. And then we have..."Ultimate Purpose" – hmmm, I can't tell if this door's ever been open – yet I suggest that you make note of it, as you'll probably want to stop back later...

Ah! Here's the door we've been looking for! "Common Sense." Welcome to your Common Sense Room. And, seeing as your door guard isn't here to let us in, please allow me to get the door...

Well, here we are... Pretty tiny, isn't it? Yet, you'll notice that there's a window – and once we draw back the curtain over this window, I assure you that it will appear much larger. In any case, now that we're here, you'll be able to make *perfect sense* of everything we've observed thus far. Yet, in order for this to happen, you are going to have to *forget* who you are...

You see, in order to make "perfect sense" of what you're about to experience, you are going to have to contemplate things from a totally *neutral* perspective. You must be willing to assume a purely unbiased point-of-view. Therefore, I encourage you to not only check "what you already know" at the door but to imagine that you've just been retained as a consultant. A consultant to *yourself.* And what kind of consultant must you be in order to make perfect sense of everything you're about to see?

Why, one with common sense, of course.

Which is precisely the perspective from which I ask that you consider your response to the following question; how are you going to prevent any negative feelings associated with your bad trophies from overshadowing the positive emotions you'd otherwise expect to feel once you begin to spend more time in your Good Trophy Room? Do you honestly believe that you can simply forget what you know about the size and content of your Bad Trophy Room?

Well, on the chance that your mind is playing tricks on you, I know of no better way to refresh your memory than to draw back the curtain over this window. For as you're about to see, your Common Sense Room just happens to be located directly next door to your Bad Trophy Room. Given which, if you simply imagine yourself giving this curtain a tug - - There she is! Look familiar?

Although I'm sure that it does, I request that you visualize it specifically as it would appear from this window – situated above and behind it all – from where you are able to look down upon the entire room at once. From this vantage point, please take a few moments to imagine how everything you observed the last time you were here would appear from this perspective. As you do, allow yourself to reflect upon how much this room has affected your life. *All* of the times you held yourself back. *All* of the times you settled for less than you deserved. Go ahead, take your time – and take it all in. And yet, even as you do so from a "neutral perspective," still allow yourself to recall how you felt whenever you earned another bad trophy and had to go into this room to put it away…

* * * * * * * * * * * * * * * * * *

Coaching; Although it's important for you to recall any pain you may have felt, it is not necessary for you to actually feel the pain; as the outcome is to simply observe that you do not enjoy visiting this room and that there is no reason to continue to do so…

* * * * * * * * * * * * * * * * * *

Remember, even as an "unbiased consultant" you must stand in your client's shoes in order to offer meaningful advice – so please allow yourself to be present to what you feel as you gaze through this window. Notice all the trophy cases and all the bad trophies, including *the biggies.* Just how "not good enough" have you been? What is the full measure of your futility? In fact, even from this perspective, can you honestly imagine being able to earn enough good trophies to ever offset all the negativity you see before you?

Given the name of the room we're observing from, I'll accept that you answered "no," which brings me to my next, and most important, question:

> For what reason would you ever want to go back into this room or want to retain any of your bad trophies?

Again, I'm soliciting your unbiased opinion as a "common sense consultant." So, I ask you, if you had a choice – and you *do* – what would you recommend doing with all of the trophies in this room, as well as with the room itself?

As you consider what *you* would do, please allow me to reveal what "consultant Jason" suggested as we contemplated his gymnasium-sized collection of bad trophies through the window of his Common Sense Room - -

"Burn it," he declared. "Burn *everything.*"

Not surprisingly, Jason's solution was swift and certain. Yet, what would you suggest? Perhaps your recommendation would be a little less volatile, yet wouldn't you want to somehow do away with this room? Wouldn't you want to somehow *disappear* all your bad trophies?

Now, as you, the consultant, continue to ponder your "common sense" solution, do you notice that *your mind* is having second thoughts? Remember, I warned you that the little guy would not take kindly to you messing with the status quo, so you can imagine how he's reacting to any talk of you shutting down *his* Bad Trophy Room.

And even though he's not allowed in here, you can be sure that he's just outside in the hallway pleading his case through the door. In light of which, can you "hear" him begging you to reconsider? Can you "feel" him trying to convince you that a fire may not be in your best interest? And isn't he somehow suggesting that no matter what you may be planning, it would be foolish to think that you'd be able to "survive" without a Bad Trophy Room?

Of course he is – which is why I encouraged you to contemplate your solution from a neutral perspective – *free of his influence.* So, from both that perspective and the vantage point of this window, please gaze once more upon that collection of misperceptions about your past and tell me, in all honesty, why would you ever want to retain any of it? What reason could you possibly have for visiting your Bad Trophy Room ever again? Remember, we're not talking about doing away with either your memory or your conscience, *only your bad trophies!*

Think about it. The only reason to re-visit this room would be to partake of an activity that in no way serves either yourself or others. And then, once inside, all that there is to do is to reminisce about "bad times." Does this make any sense at all? If you didn't have to go back in there, why would you? So again, I ask: what would you advise yourself to do with this room and all the trophies?

Well, we definitely know what Jason would do, yet I have conducted this process with hundreds of other clients – so allow me to reveal what a few of them suggested. Interestingly, their careers seemed to influence their recommendations…

Craig, the General Contractor: *Brick it up.*

Carole, the Executive Assistant: *Shred it.*

Cynthia, the Relocation Specialist: *Move it somewhere else.*

Karen, the Actress: *Write it out of the script.*

Shelton, the Attorney: *Have it condemned and bulldozed.*
Matthew, the Investment Banker: *Liquidate everything and close it down!*

By the way, although just about everyone who has ever participated in this process has benefitted immensely, Matthew seemed to appreciate it more than most. In fact, as of this writing, he is the reigning "Trophy King," which is what I crowned him the day we stepped into his Good Trophy Room and discovered *hundreds* of trophies already in there! Yet, even his Bad Trophy Room dwarfed his good one, so he was delighted with the prospect of "liquidating all of his bad trophies and closing the place down."

So, have you decided what to do with *your* Bad Trophy Room?

Well, whatever you do, I implore you to pay no attention to that little man throwing the tantrum in the hallway. Obviously, he has no appreciation for the fact that shutting down your Bad Trophy Room would have a tremendous impact on your psychology – because it's just as obvious that he's a "one track mind" when it comes to steering you clear of threats to your survival. And, from *his* perspective, any attempt to do away with your Bad Trophy Room would be just that. Which, of course, explains the tantrum.

Still, although we knew he'd be upset, what's the big deal *really?* After all, it's not as though he'd be out of work, given that he spends most of his time guarding your good room anyway – and you're certainly not going to do away with *that* room anytime soon. So, what is it about your Bad Trophy Room that he doesn't seem to think he can live without?

Well, actually, it's *two* things. Both of which you should be aware of so that after you close this room down, you won't be tempted to re-open it when he shows up begging you to do so. Which, I promise you, *he will.* At least until he's satisfied that you're surviving just fine without your Bad Trophy Room…

As you'll recall, whenever the mind perceives a threat, it immediately initiates a search of your *past* to determine if you've encountered a similar threat before. Why? Because if you did and you're still here, you obviously *survived.* In which case, because the action your mind prompted you to take *that last time* must have done the trick, it's going to compel you to take an identical action *this time* in order to survive you through your current situation.

And where do you suppose your mind is going to look in order to determine how it survived you through a similar threat "that last time?"

That's right – in your Bad Trophy Room! And, if you take another look through this window at all your bad trophies, you'll understand why…

So, what do you see? Yes, I know – lots of proof that you're not good enough (which is, of course, why you'll be "closing the place down" very soon). Yet, what else is true about everything you see in that room? What *else* did you "do" in spite of whatever you did to earn those trophies? In every one of those moments where you fell short or otherwise proved to yourself that you weren't good enough, what else also happened?

Right again – you *survived!* Every time. In spite of not being good enough and in spite of falling short time and time again, you still lived to tell the tale!!!

Therefore, can you see that whenever the mind awards a trophy in honor of you not being good enough, it's likewise recognizing the fact that you survived the incident? In which case, not only are the trophies in your Bad Trophy Room "proof" that you're not good enough, they are also proof that, in spite of not being good enough, you survived!!!

And whose duty is it to ensure your survival? Who must have done their job each and every time you earned a trophy and then survived long enough to store it your Bad Trophy Room? That's right; the door guard. Your *mind.*

Thus, isn't it likely that although the mind does award bad trophies as proof that you're not good enough, who the mind is actually recognizing with the trophy is the one who pulled you through in spite of you not being good enough – which is, of course, *itself?* Thus, can you see that the mind is *really* collecting trophies on its own behalf and not yours? In fact, isn't this the more "common sense" explanation?

Of course it is. Yet, for what reason would the mind award itself trophies?

Well, it certainly did its job, didn't it? In fact, didn't it do *two* jobs? Didn't it both "prove you not good enough" and, in spite of that, "survive you" all at once? Seems pretty trophy-worthy to me. As a matter of fact, I'm surprised the little guy didn't give himself two of them!

In any case, can you see that the mind has not been awarding *you* trophies after all? Surely, it's been awarding them in recognition *of* you for not being good enough, but it wasn't awarding them *to* you. It's been awarding them *to itself* for a job well done. For surviving you! For being your hero! For pulling you through time and time again!!

Given this, can you see that this isn't even your trophy room? It's the mind's "ego" room. And although you adopted it and have always considered it yours, it is, in fact, the mind's "good" trophy room – which is why the little fellow is not exactly thrilled with the prospect of you closing it down.

So, now that you know that this isn't your room, should you not feel bad anymore? Well, although it would be nice if it worked this way, even though you are now aware that you are not really putting one of your bad trophies into your bad room, do you notice that you don't feel any better about it? After all, whether it's your *bad* trophy or the mind's *good* trophy, it's still a trophy that got awarded in recognition of an incident where *you* fell short. Therefore, no matter whose room it is, it's still overflowing with trophies that have your name on them, which means that you still feel the pain whenever you go in there.

In which case, let the closing ceremonies begin!!!

But don't expect your door guard to be there – unless, of course, he shows up in protest. For as you now know, he's not about to give in until he's certain you mean business. At which point, he will get over it. He will survive…

After all, that's his job.

"Reflect upon your present blessings, of which every man has many – not on your past misfortunes, of which all men have some…"

-Charles Dickens

* * * * * * * * * * * * * * * * * *

Coaching; ***You are not your mind!*** *Please be very clear about what you just observed. Notice that when you (the Self) step into your Bad Trophy Room, you feel pain – yet whenever your mind steps into this very same room, it feels validated and vindicated. Hence, there exists a very obvious distinction between your Self (intention) and your Mind (survival).*

* * * * * * * * * * * * * * * * * *

Notes -

Chapter 15 - *Locking the Door and Throwing Away the Key*

In the absence of this being something that most people would consider common knowledge, just how does one go about closing down a Bad Trophy Room?

Well, the first step is to acknowledge having created it in the first place. To which end, are you willing to admit that no one coerced you into filling up your bad room or prevented you from filling up your good room? Are you able to see that both of these rooms exist as they do because of *you?* Once you are clear that it was you who created these rooms in the first place, you will know that you have the power to *re*-create them as you'd like them to be.

Shutting down your Bad Trophy Room is simply an expression of your desire and *intention.* You've always had the power to close this room down. You just didn't know it. Heck, you didn't even know you had one! But once you acknowledge your power, it's actually just a matter of making it happen. In fact, just as soon as you're convinced that it's the right thing to do, this room and all of your bad trophies will be nothing more than a distant memory…

However, if you are of the concern that this room provides some form of value that may show up as missing "down the road," or if you feel that you might otherwise regret shutting it down, then you could be a little uneasy about letting it go.

So, which is it? Are you still on the fence or are you ready to take back control of your life by locking the door and throwing away the key?

Well, if you are having second thoughts about closing down this room, are you willing to acknowledge that it's the little man throwing the fit in the hallway who has reeled you in? Remember, he's a very *sneaky* fellow! In fact, he's an expert at causing you to doubt yourself, while at the same time having you believe that *he* has nothing to do with it – which is why very few of us are able to perceive his influence. Instead, we are convinced that we are "thinking for ourselves." That we are simply being *prudent.*

Therefore, even if you have come to the conclusion that it makes perfect sense to do so, it wouldn't at all be unusual for you to still be unsure about shutting down this room. In light of which (and in support of you being able to make the "right" decision), it will serve you to acknowledge how much your indecisiveness is being driven by one or more of the following concerns:

* Conscience; for what if we become *so free* that we abandon all consideration of what is right or wrong, or our social morés in general?

* Humility; for what if we grow so "full of ourselves" that no one can stand us?

* Loss of connection with an existing relationship or peer group; for what if *we* change, but "they" don't? What if we become open and happier, yet those with whom we are in relationship do not?

* Fear of the unknown; for what if living without a bad trophy room is just too scary? What if we actually were unleashed or had no boundaries?

* Survival (the biggie); for where would the mind look to determine how to survive us through a threat? How would it know what to do? After all, we have survived pretty well thus far. Perhaps the mind really does know what's best…

There you go. Maybe your mind knows what's best. And just who do you suppose is thinking *that* thought? The Self – or the *mind?* Remember, from the mind's perspective, you are not good enough to overcome any of these "what ifs" – which would confirm that these are its reasons for not wanting to let go of your Bad Trophy Room, not yours!

In any event, you can never consciously shut down your *memory.* So even after doing away with all your bad trophies (including the associated evidence that you're not good enough), you'll still be able to recall those incidents. Meaning that you'll also be able to recall and apply any lessons you may have learned while surviving them (which you can employ either as motivation or to help you avoid making similar mistakes in the future).

No matter how much you have ever felt unworthy or wanted to quit, it was never because of your *bad memories,* but because those memories lived within your trophy room as proof that you weren't good enough – and it's the "proof that you're not good enough" part that you'll soon be giving up. From which point forward, those memories will live as nothing more than what they are; as *memories* rather than "proof." Except, perhaps, as proof that you are human, which we'll be exploring shortly…

Ultimately, it's your call as to whether you live *intentionally* or *in reaction,* as your mind will forever have access to all your memories. Therefore, if you're okay with living a life that is little more than a regurgitated version of your past, you'll still be able to do so. If you would rather play it safe and "itsy-bitsy" yourself toward your future, no one can force you to take more chances. And, if it serves you to live solely at the effect of your conscience rather than in alignment with a grander vision or purpose, then by all means, please do.

You see, once you let go of your Bad Trophy Room, you'll still have every option you ever had – *except* the option to award yourself bad trophies. Yet this would be a problem because…???

Otherwise, with regard to any lingering concern that you will somehow regret the loss of your Bad Trophy Room, I invite you to simply let this go. Give it up. I assure you that you will not turn into an arrogant jerk as a result of letting go of the belief that you're not good enough. Nor will you become so full of yourself that you'll forget about everyone else.

In fact, as you come to experience yourself as "whole and complete," you are much more likely to focus your attention on others as you also come to realize that you're able to bring forth even greater empathy. What's more, you are certainly not going to quit your job or risk all of your savings on some foolhardy investment just because you are no longer controlled by the failures of your past.

After all, I am in no way suggesting that you give up either your *intelligence* or your *common sense* – only your bad trophies!

So, are you ready to let it go? Are you prepared to shut down your Bad Trophy Room and to quit proving to yourself that you're not good enough? Well, if you've answered *yes* – and you mean it, then it's already done. *It's gone!!*

Of course, I could say "poof" if that would make you feel any better – but that might imply that we've worked some kind of magic when, in fact, there is nothing at all magical about doing away with one's Bad Trophy Room. Letting it go is nothing more than a function of your intention to break free of both your *mind* and your *social conditioning*.

You see, there's no way that one can live both intentionally and from survival at the same time. So once you "speak yourself" with *certainty* and *conviction* (thereby declaring to the universe that you are going to show up a certain way simply because you *say* so), then *that* is "living with intention." Once you make this declaration and refuse to accept any more bad trophies, you *won't* – and when you decide to stay out of your Bad Trophy Room, you *will!*

Even so, your mind isn't likely to "retire" anytime soon, so I can assure you that your door guard will still attempt to intervene every time he perceives a threat. But from now on, you'll have the ability to simply ignore him for two very good reasons;

1) **Because you <u>are</u> good enough!** In fact, we are *all* good enough – and even though we all share the same perceptions and illusions that drive our fears, you and I are ***whole and***

complete and magnificent beyond our wildest imaginations! Thus, you *are* worthy and must no longer accept trophies that suggest otherwise.

2) **Because you don't have to!!** Again, you only ever submitted to any of this because you had no clue. But now you know that you possess the power to ***just say no!!***

"You can drop your personal history right now. Just drop it. What you need is a teacher to teach you that you have immeasurable power within you."

–Wayne Dyer

Still, you are human. Thus, you can never break totally free of the minds inclination to ensure your survival and you will likely continue to experience at least some degree of fear in the face of taking action toward a desired outcome. What's more, I assure you that you will still make mistakes and will sometimes do things you wish you hadn't. However, none of this is proof that you're not good enough; it's simply proof that you are human.

In fact, unless you decide to dig yourself a hole and hide out forever, you are pretty much guaranteed to experience "falling short" on a fairly regular basis.

In baseball, even the best hitter's fall short at least six out of every ten times at bat. During his basketball career, Michael Jordan missed far more potential game winning shots than he made. Even Thomas Edison failed to invent the light bulb more than a thousand times before he finally "saw the light." So, unless you really do itsy-bitsy yourself through the rest of your life, you will undoubtedly fall short a lot more often than not. But even when you do, the only thing that this will prove is that you are just like everyone else; *human.*

Therefore, falling short is proof of nothing more than you haven't succeeded yet.

So, my human friend, now that you've given up access to your Bad Trophy Room, what are you going to do the next time you perceive a threat, fall short, make a mistake, or are otherwise afraid that you aren't good enough? Well, for one thing, you'll now have the option of doing what other "awake" and transformed beings do when they come face-to-face with their humanity. *Nothing.*

That's right. Nothing. For once you recognize and honor the distinction between your *Self* and your *mind,* and then consciously decide to close down your Bad Trophy Room, the ability to do "nothing" shows up as a wholly viable option. Which means that from now on, you will be able to choose to "do nothing" rather than "react out of survival" – at least until you formulate an intentional, intelligent, and appropriate response.

In other words, the next time you feel a threat, you'll be able to simply observe and *let go of* your instinctual compulsion to react from fear (rather than allowing your mind to offer up a survival response from your past). After which, you'll be inclined to move toward your outcome or a resolution in an intentional and purposeful manner.

By doing so, you'll be empowered to let things go rather than award yourself a bad trophy (which is a good thing, because you'll no longer have anywhere to put it). Again, now that you're aware of the power of "Being," you'll have the ability to choose to react *intentionally* rather than from a compulsion to prove that you are good enough in the face of a concern that you are not. At which point, you'll be free to simply "be."

Still, as refreshing as this may sound, it may take some getting used to – as your mind has long enjoyed awarding you bad trophies versus "letting things go." Yet, I assure you that training yourself to *let things go* will not be as difficult as you might think.

And why is that? For the simple reason that you've actually been *letting things go* your entire life. And, as a result, you are already a virtual expert at doing so!

After all, have you forgotten why there are so few trophies in your Good Trophy Room? That's right – because you almost never award yourself good trophies when you deserve them. You know perfectly well that you've done lots of good things in your life and lots of good things have happened to you – yet you've become extremely proficient at not fully acknowledging either these incidents or yourself. Instead, you've chosen to "let things go."

Consequently, nothing but *your mind* stands between you and letting go of anything for which you would have previously awarded yourself a bad trophy. You've already built the muscle – yet rarely applied it on the negative side.

However, now that you are aware that you've been letting go unconsciously and routinely on the good side, you'll be able to do so *consciously* and *intentionally* on the bad side; whenever you choose!!

Thus is revealed the fourth premise of *The Trophy Effect,* which is that you already possess the capacity to let things go (as clearly demonstrated by your relatively meager collection of good trophies) and that this ability, when applied in conjunction with the other three premises, establishes a foundation from which you will be empowered to evolve a more self-forgiving and positive psychology.

In light of this fourth premise, are you ready and willing to let things go? Are you prepared to give up not only all of your bad trophies but all of your reasons for not awarding yourself good ones? Are you ready to construct a brand new future around "the truth of your magnificence" rather than continue to live your life in the shadow of the concern that you're not good enough?

After all, you already know enough to qualify as an authority on both *survival* and the Daisy Chain, and could undoubtedly conduct a lecture on all four premises of *The Trophy Effect.* What's more, you have witnessed first-hand how your Bad Trophy Room got so full and why your Good Trophy Room did not – and you're also aware of what that "little man" does behind the curtain when he's not standing guard at the door.

And yet, in order to extract all the value you deserve from the remainder of our journey, you must be willing to acknowledge the extent to which you have been *unconsciously influenced* by the effect of "social conditioning." To own up to the fact that your "subconscious, culturally-instilled, evaluation filter" would have rendered it virtually impossible for you to have contemplated these last fifteen chapters from anywhere other than the confines of your fishbowl.

For even though you may have been inspired to break free of your *cultural conditioning* for a few random moments at a time, it's unlikely that you would have interpreted anything you've read thus far from a perspective other than the one from which you perceive everything else – which is through the "filter" of your socially-conditioned point-of-view. In other words, from the perspective that most everyone else (the culture) would consider a "normal" or "traditional" manner of thinking.

Still, having read this far, you have likely attained the first half of the outcome I promised you back in Chapter One – which was that by the time you finished reading this book you'd have come to know all of this from both a traditional *and* a transformed perspective. Therefore, if I'm to make good on the second half of my promise, it will be necessary for us to re-evaluate things from a *transformed* point-of-view.

And since I have every intention of keeping this promise, that's precisely what we will be doing over the course of the next few chapters, as we are about to examine not only how you and I think in general, but where we think *from.* In other words, we are about to explore what it is that shapes our thinking <u>beyond</u> *The Trophy Effect.*

In advance of which, I invite you to consider that since most of what you've already learned about the content of your fishbowl you were not even aware that you didn't know before reading this book, wouldn't it be reasonable to assume that there are other things you may still not know?

Trusting that you're okay with this assumption, I encourage you to fully embrace this possibility, as we are about to explore the very nature of our thinking – *and the universe* – from this perspective. In fact, what lies before you is not only the opportunity to discover something you may not already know, but the opportunity to re-think everything you *do* know from a much more "enlightened" perspective.

In light of which, you might as well be prepared to kiss your fishbowl goodbye…

"To find yourSelf, think for yourSelf."

-Socrates

Notes -

Chapter 16 - *Out of the Fishbowl and into the Cosmos*

"We are what we think. All that we are arises with our thoughts. With our thoughts we make our world."

–Buddha

Now that you are aware that you have the ability to "just say no" to accepting any more bad trophies, I assure you that you'll soon be collecting good trophies by the dozen and spending as much quality time in the Good Trophy Room as your heart desires!

However, in advance of sending you off into the world in search of these trophies, I encourage you to put everything you *already know* on hold – as we're about to explore both the grander objecttive behind this search and the extent to which all of us have been unwittingly influenced by our culturally-instilled beliefs and considerations. During which, you will likely find what you "already know" to be of very little use…

Needless to say, once you begin to focus on the positive aspects of your life rather than on the negative aspects, you'll likely feel a whole lot better than before. Still, there's a much higher purpose to be realized via the quest for good trophies beyond simply feeling better. After all, if the only wisdom I had to impart was that you should spend *less* time in your Bad Trophy Room feeling crappy and *more* time in your Good Trophy Room feeling happy, I probably could have done so in half as many chapters.

Instead, we've just put the wraps on a fifteen-chapter odyssey that was designed to inspire specific insights and to evoke pertinent realizations – not only for the purpose of maximizing your understanding of *The Trophy Effect* – but to allow you to observe that things are *not always* as they appear to be. In light of which, I'm not at all interested in you simply "feeling better" – as that wouldn't even be worthy of the time it's taken you to read this book.

Rather, it is my intention that you experience nothing less than a massive shift in your sense of *Self* ("Being"); hence, a *quantum shift* in your psychology, that will enable you to be more fully present to the truth of your magnificence and newly empowered to live each day as passionately as possible!

In fact, I trust that you've already realized a substantial shift in your level of *awareness.* For unless your mind was able to convince you to fully disregard all fifteen chapters – or unless you had previously come to know any of this by some other means – you now know far more about human nature than you ever did before.

Yet, as previously alluded to, wouldn't it be fair to say that most of what you've learned thus far has to do with things that you didn't even know that you didn't know?

You see, the "things we don't know" fall into two categories. There are things that we know we don't know, such as how to rebuild an automobile engine, do the tango, or get a teenager to do their homework. Then, there are those things that we *don't even know* we don't know – which are things that don't even show up as missing in our lives due to the power of ***social conditioning***.

Essentially, it's as a result of "social conditioning" that we perceive or experience things as we *expect* them to be rather than as they really are. Typically, these are notions or presumptions that so thoroughly permeate the culture that we never think to question them. Things that we not only take for granted, but are quick to defend should anyone else call them into question – even if we've never conducted any form of *personal* investigation or confirmed their validity in any way.

For centuries, human beings were socially conditioned to accept that the Earth was flat. After all, *anyone* could see that this was true. So, when Columbus set off in search of the New World, most everyone believed that he would fall off the edge. Of course, that didn't happen because the truth is the truth whether you believe it or not. Yet, unless you expect to see the truth, you won't – as we typically only ever see what we expect to see.

For example, upon landing in the Americas, Columbus was able to sail directly into the harbor undetected by the natives, who had no idea that he had arrived until his crew disembarked from their larger ships and rowed ashore in smaller boats. Why? Because they had never seen ships as large as the Santa Maria – nor even considered that ships like these existed; thus, they were not *conditioned* to perceive them. Of course, the natives had all seen tiny boats before, so they had no problem perceiving what they *expected* to see.

How strong of a force is social conditioning? Well, we've all heard of Galileo, who was threatened with death for suggesting that the Sun did *not* revolve around the Earth. Thankfully, most societies have evolved to the degree that they no longer forbid or condemn this kind of thinking; yet, neither are they quick to embrace discoveries that tend to contradict the prevailing reality – especially when our senses perceive a thing to be a certain way in the face of a revelation that would tend to disprove that assumption.

For instance, if America's founding fathers declared that we have the right to *pursue* happiness, then who are we to question whether or not happiness is something that must be pursued? Yet this notion, I suggest, is one that our forefathers shared as a result of *social conditioning;* the very same notion that gave rise to the third premise of *The Trophy Effect* – which, as you recall, is that good trophies are special and extremely rare.

Therefore, prior to being able to award yourself good trophies on a more consistent basis, you must be willing to separate yourself from this "cultural misperception." You must first be willing to acknowledge that you have, in fact, aligned with this notion and have been living your life as if it were true (at least for the most part).

You see, most of us assume that "being happy" or "having fun" is beyond our direct control. If we attend a social gathering, the best we can do is to "hope" that we'll have a good time. We hope that if the right people are there and if the right things happen, then maybe we'll enjoy ourselves. We believe that happiness will show up only if something *causes* it to (or, perhaps, if we have a few cocktails or otherwise artificially alter our consciousness).

In fact, this is nothing but an illusion born of social conditioning, in that there is nothing outside of yourself that can *make* you happy. The reality is that happiness has as much to do with one's state of consciousness and ***expectations*** with regard to what happens as it does with what actually happens. Therefore, when you both expect to be happy and do <u>not</u> consider happiness to exist beyond the realm of your personal creation, it is entirely possible to experience being happy *at will.*

However, if you believe that happiness is *elusive*, then that's precisely how it will show up – or not show up – as the case may be…

"I am happy and content because I think I am."

–Alain Rene Lesage

A simple example of this "expectation phenomenon" may be found in the story of "the wandering German Shepherd" – which had been strolling along a street one day when it noticed an open door. As it turned out, this door lead directly into the lobby of a grand hotel where dozens of people were sitting around waiting for whatever people wait for in hotel lobbies. As the dog wandered in wagging its tail, a few of the patrons became startled and were quick to move away, while others were just as quick to whisper "good doggie" as they reached out to pet it…

So, was the German Shepherd a threat or a treat? Annoying or entertaining? Frightening or a "good doggie"? In fact, all the German Shepherd did was "do" German Shepherd. It wasn't any of these things *inherently.* It simply *did what it did* and the patrons *got what they got* or *saw what they saw* – and what they saw was what they expected to see. Simply put, the "dog did dog" and the observer's *personal conditioning* did the rest.

Are you able to see how this force has affected you? As you've likely noticed over the course of our journey, *all* of us have been influenced by personal and social conditioning in ways too numerous to count. Yet, with specific regard to *The Trophy Effect,* we've been culturally-conditioned to believe that happiness is something that must be pursued, that it is "right" to be humble and "wrong" to blow our own horn, and that "toned down" is an acceptable and viable alternative to playing full out.

What's more, when presented with either the opportunity or the need to make a decision, we are inclined to believe that our only viable option is "one or the other" (either/or), as it's implausible to assume that we could ever have things *both* ways.

In fact, even the basic premise that we are not good enough is an outgrowth of our social conditioning, as it is spawned solely by the perception that you and I exist as fully independent Selves. Yet the truth (although impossible to perceive from within our fishbowl) is that we are all inextricably connected at the most fundamental level of consciousness – thus, there is no "separate Self" – nor are we inherently greater or lesser than anyone or anything else. As such, once you are able to step outside of your fishbowl and experience yourself as inseparable from "that which creates it all" (Source / Divine Energy / God), the fear that you are somehow lesser or not good enough disappears!

Until then, we dance with this fear against the backdrop of *the grand illusion,* which is that you and I are thoroughly independent entities that are in no way connected to anyone or anything else. Hence, we are quick to dismiss our similarities and rarely allow ourselves to experience this connectedness, primarily because we do not expect any such connectedness to exist. Consequently, we often feel lonely or fearful – even in the presence of other human beings.

Again, as an outgrowth of social conditioning, our senses perceive this "separateness" simply because we *expect* to see things in this manner. After all, you and I certainly appear to exist as separate selves (just as the Earth appeared to be flat), thus we've been conditioned to perceive that "consciousness" is uniquely personal and is something that emanates from within our *local* mind. However, the notion that "who you are" is a fully independent Self – hence, the source of your own personal consciousness – is nothing more than an illusion on par with the notion than the Earth is flat or that Columbus's ships were never really anchored in that harbor.

In fact, who and what we are is *pure consciousness*. Everything is pure consciousness. We are fully and completely connected at the level of pure consciousness to everything else. Thus, we are actually "one" with everything and inseparable from the cosmic intelligence "which creates it all." Hence, we are all inherently and equally whole and complete in every moment!

Even so, it's highly unlikely that you'll be able to perceive things in this manner unless you allow yourself to think from "outside the box" – or, I should say, from outside the fishbowl. As you've likely noticed, neither "oneness" nor "pure consciousness" make sense from a socially-conditioned perspective – thus, they cannot possibly be experienced from within a fishbowl filled with *separateness* and *objectivity* (an "I am over here / you are over there" based perception of reality); which is how we perceive the universe when we consider ourselves to exist as fully distinct from that universe.

Consequently, in order for you to experience things as they *really* are, you're going to have to leave your fishbowl behind…

So, are you ready and willing to do that? Have you been able to *un*-condition yourself sufficiently over the course of our journey to finally step beyond your fishbowl?

Once you do (thereby conceding that the existing neural-connections within your brain are aligned with your social conditioning rather than in alignment with "the way things really are"), you will have opened the door to a universe where you have the ability to create things exactly as you'd like them to be.

You and I have access to unlimited power, yet once we assumed that we were separate from *Source* (from universal intelligence), we then gave up that power and now feel helpless in the face of our circumstances – but only because we experience these circumstances as having been created by something separate from ourselves.

Surely, I do not expect you to master these distinctions nor become enlightened or proficient in quantum mechanics over the next few chapters. Likewise, there's no need for you to become either a guru or a physicist in order to observe how these principles apply to *The Trophy Effect.*

Still, these principles are likely to play havoc with your existing concept of reality if you attempt to make sense of them from your socially-conditioned point-of-view. Therefore, I suggest that you begin the process of breaking free of your conditioning by putting what you "already know" on the shelf – thereby allowing these next few chapters to speak to that part of you that longs to know it*Self*...

To be sure, even as you step willingly out of your fishbowl, it may take some time for your "eyes to adjust" to these distinctions. Hence, the "secret" to coming to know all that we are about to explore is that you must be willing to embrace it *before* you see it, as it is unlikely that you will ever come to know "oneness" if you are unwilling to embrace it until *after* you see it or understand it.

Once you surrender into a "faithful knowing" (which is distinct from *believing*) that you are inseparable from everything else, you will find yourself expecting to see expressions of this in everyone and everything – at which point, you *will* be able to see them.

However, if you are having difficulty observing these expressions, it's more than likely because you have not yet broken free of your social conditioning, which is preventing you from perceiving anything you are *not* expecting to see. Of course, in order to break free of your social conditioning, you must first be willing to step beyond your fishbowl. Yet, how – you may be wondering – are you going to step beyond your fishbowl without first breaking free of your social conditioning?

Obviously, if there was a simple answer, everyone would be enlightened!

In any case, if you've not yet "cracked this code," do not be dismayed – as "God's delays are not God's denials." By staying the course, it will come to you in time – as we've only begun to explore these distinctions from outside the fishbowl. That is, from the perspective of the *Self,* which is fully awake to the fact that "who you are" is *pure consciousness* and inseparable from *Source.*

Again, although I recommend that you continue reading with the intention to ultimately "master" these distinctions, it is certainly not necessary for you to *be* a Master in order to extract maximum value from the remainder of this book. Even so, I suggest that you remain open and willing to embrace the truth when it reveals itself to you. For if you are determined to break free of your fishbowl, *you will!* And, even though you may not "wake up" fully transformed or enlightened after digesting nothing other than these final few chapters, it is my intention that you at least wake up to the fact that *enlightenment* is not only your birthright – it is fully within your grasp – and that you are, in fact, moving in that direction.

Then, once you embrace this possibility and complete the exercises in Chapter Nineteen, you will be poised to continue down this path with *The Trophy Effect* finally working *for* you rather than against you…

In the mean time, as we continue to explore our inherent connectedness, wholeness, and magnificence, I implore you to check your social conditioning at the door – for only then will it be possible for you to experience yourself *as one with it all* – at which point you'll be able to see for yourself that the world is not flat…

Chapter 17 - *"The Truth"*

"Oh God, help me believe in the truth about myself,
no matter how beautiful it is. Amen."

-Macrina Wiederkehr

Well, have you done it? Have you checked your fishbowl at the door?

If so, you will finally be able to experience yourself as I described you in Chapter Fifteen; as ***whole and complete and magnificent beyond your wildest imagination!***

Again, the only reason you've been unable to recognize this before now is that your social conditioning wouldn't let you. Remember, when living inside your fishbowl, you could only see what you were *conditioned* to see – and you were never conditioned to experience yourself as whole and complete. You didn't expect it, so you couldn't see it.

However, in the absence of your old conditioning, you will be empowered to embrace your universal "being-ness" (your Self), which is naturally free of any concern that you are lacking anything at all. And, if you aren't "lacking anything at all," what are you? You are whole and complete, right? And wouldn't that be pretty magnificent?

In actuality, there is *nothing* that you are not.

Every inclination you've ever felt to react from fear was nothing more than an outgrowth of your inherited cultural conditioning, which gave rise to the illusion that you are somehow separate from the *universal intelligence* that creates it all; an outgrowth of the superstition that *who you are* is a separate Self, distinct from other Selves. This is the source of all fear.

Given which, a more accurate way of describing the fear of not being good enough is as an outgrowth of having aligned with the notion that you are separate from everything else – including love and courage. Therefore, an equally accurate assertion would be that the fears which prompt *The Trophy Effect* are not inherent human fears, but inherent fishbowl fears.

And although you are now fully capable of seeing this illusion for what it is and are prepared to push through any fear or limiting belief to do so, it wouldn't at all be unusual for you to be feeling a little bit of lingering uncertainty. A little bit of "wonder." If so, please do not confuse this feeling with *fear,* as this is nothing other than the *sense of anticipation* that tends to show up whenever a "whole and complete" human being takes on anything of consequence for the very first time (such as stepping beyond ones fishbowl).

For instance, no matter how long or hard a runner has trained for their first marathon, it's a pretty sure bet that they will notice this *wonder* as they lace up their running shoes on race day. And even if a physician has graduated from medical school with Honors, this same sense of wonder will likely show up the moment he or she begins to examine their very first patient…

So, even though you are now an "expert" on human nature, have given up your Bad Trophy Room, and have learned the truth about your *oneness* with the universe, it's only natural that you would wonder how you are going to apply all of this or how it will affect your life. Yet, I assure you that it will all work out as it should, so I invite you to simply notice this "wonder" – and *let it go...*

Again, the fact that you're feeling a bit uncertain is not at all unusual. After all, you're about to step back into your life with a brand new psychology and a whole new way of experiencing the universe (free of your fishbowl). Consequently, it may take a while for you to master "doing nothing" (as opposed to reacting from fear) and you are going to have to get used to acknowledging and rewarding your own magnificence (as well as acknowledging and rewarding others). In consideration of which, I'm certainly not going to send you off into the world without any training.

In Chapter Nineteen, you will be shifting from "learning" into "being," by way of a series of fun and powerful exercises that will allow you to apply all of this "in the real world." As promised, you will discover how to re-think and modify your Good Trophy Room rules and guidelines, meaning that it won't be long before you are awarding good trophies by the truckload! At which point, you'll simply have to put up with being happy more often!

And although "being happy more often" is certainly a worthy objective, the primary purpose of these Exercises is to enable you to intentionally (and repeatedly) override your reactive mind; a process that will empower you to break free of your social conditioning and allow you to see things as they *really* are.

By simply following these Exercises, the perception of yourself as separate from everyone and everything else will begin to melt away and, although your actions may seem a bit contrived at first, the *Self* will soon "kick in." Eventually, it will all begin to snowball until, at some point, you will come to realize that your fishbowl has been smashed to smithereens; leaving you fully present to your own magnificence – as well as the magnificence of others. Which, in actuality, is one and the same.

Once this occurs, you will begin to be present to the force within you that is "doing" your intentional thinking; the "force" that has *always* been there but has been obscured by your fishbowl until now. How did this happen? Well, you "learned it." You learned it by trusting your senses. It looked a certain way, so you believed it. After all, it certainly appears that "who we are" is separate from one another, so it would follow that "who you are" would be located *within* your physical body. Therefore, you and I assumed this to be true. At which moment the *ego* was born – as was our compulsion to feed it.

Once you assumed that "who you are" was located within your body, your mind decided that it needed *to survive* your body and made that its number one priority. Unfortunately, the need for your mind to survive your body was realized at the expense of your grander experience of *Self.* Thus, you were never permitted access to that grander vision of your Universal Self (Source / Divine Energy / God); that which was here before you showed up as a specific incarnation of matter (your body) and *that* which will be here long after that body disintegrates back into the tiny particles of energy from which it emerged.

Who we really are is the intention and intelligence *behind* that which caused us to show up in the first place, not that which showed up. We are *one* with that intention. In fact, everything is manifested from this *Source,* which encompasses everything that is and ever was. What's more, everything that ever was, still is – and always will be. It simply changes form – and these changes only appear to be linear or progressive because you and I tend to believe that we exist as a fixed point-of-view from which we perceive these forms. Yet this is an illusion, as these forms exist as *all* forms, and all at the same time.

In other words, who you are is *pure potentiality,* which arises from a field of universal consciousness – which is *forever.* If you identify with that which dies (the body), you will feel fear – yet if you align with the truth (Divine consciousness), which is eternal, you will feel *freedom.* At which point, you will know that who you *really* are, does not die – and you will know this intuitively without ever having had this thought…

Speaking of thoughts, just who do you think is doing your *intentional* thinking?

Well, another illusion strikes again; for although you may argue that *you* are wholly responsible for your most creative thoughts, the truth is that "they" are thinking you. More precisely, *that* which was here before you showed up thinks *through* you. Thus, whenever you are thinking *on purpose* and with an *intention* to make a difference, you are "*being* thought" – which is what I am experiencing as I write this, as I am clear that these are not my "own" thoughts born of any "personal consciousness" (although they are certainly shaped by my personal intention and knowing). So although my fingers are typing, the experience is that I am "being used" as the typist for *that* which is coming *through* me – yet from which I am not separate.

- - - - - - - - - - - - - - -

For example, the Wright Brothers did not invent flying – they "discovered" it – by allowing that which was necessary to enable flight to think "through" them.

- - - - - - - - - - - - - - -

However, at some point you perceived that you were separate from that which was thinking you and assumed your *Self* to be located within your body, which was being used by *that* which was thinking you. This is when it all went awry; the moment that *"that,"* which you identified as "you," decided that you were distinct from everything else. The moment you decided that *you* had a beginning and an end. The moment you decided that you were better or worse than *that* which you decided you were distinct from. In other words, the moment you (your ego) decided that you were better or worse than anything else.

You see, by buying into the social conditioning and identifying yourself as separate, you turned God into a door guard. You made "him" judgmental. You minimized him and made him small. Since you are *Source* and Source is *you,* when you experience yourself as separate from Source, you minimize your experience of Source *and* your Self.

You have been given the gift of the universe but refused to accept it, saying instead, "No thanks, I'll just have this little piece of something I'll call *me.*" Maybe you were being humble. Perhaps you didn't want to take more than your share. But now you know that you don't have to play that game. You can claim what is rightfully yours. Experience yourself as it *all* and all of it as *you.* Experience yourself *as one with Source* and allow divine energy to flow through you. Can you see that if you allowed "God" to flow through you and took responsibility for this happening, you could not possibly play small? And, as "one with Source," you could not possibly downplay your own magnificence?

Any and all actions that are in alignment with anything other than pure intention are acts that are perpetuated from the hallucination that you are separate from *Source* and everything else. In the shadow of any such actions you will feel alone and you will feel fear; *the fear that you're not good enough.* After all, if you were standing in the presence of an all-encompassing universe, yet considered your-self separate from that universe, wouldn't it be natural to feel like a little bitty speck of forgotten nothing?

If you were the only thing left out of the entire field of pure potentiality, wouldn't you feel insignificant and fearful? Yet, when you align with the truth of the oneness of it all, then you will be empowered by the realization that you are neither *alone,* nor *lesser,* than anyone or anything else.

Of course, in this same moment of realization, you will also notice that you are neither *more* nor *better* than anything else – which is a powerful and freeing experience – in that you'll no longer have the need to prove anything to anyone! Besides, whom would you be proving it to? God already knows how magnificent you are.

Therefore, I invite you to give up trying to prove it. Instead, *expect* to see it. The only reason you failed to recognize your magnificence before is because you were not expecting to see it. You thought "the world was flat" so that is what you saw. After all, that's the way it appeared because that's the hallucination you were born into (the illusion that you are not inherently whole and complete and magnificent). You never questioned it, so you bought into it – and even argued for it – and then found "proof" at every turn.

Therefore, I invite you to surrender fully into your magnificence and oneness, as only then can you *expect* to see it. Remember, the truth is the truth whether you align with it or not and the truth doesn't care whether you believe it or not. However, there is power and grace to be had in awakening to your magnificence; thereby empowering yourself to experience the truth of *what is.*

To this end, the process of acknowledging good trophies is a grand expression of the *Self,* as it seeks to align with its own magnificence and power; *the power of intention.* In the moment you consciously decide to award a good trophy, you acknowledge and honor yourself *as Source*, thereby enabling you to create the experience of privilege, gratitude, and love, which you are intentionally bringing forth on behalf of the universe – which is *you.* Not only that, but you get to feel pretty damn good as well!

> *"As an expression of its intention to manifest itSelf, Source yearns to be expressed as fully as possible. Thus, when you embrace your magnificence by either doing or acknowledging "good things," you are aligning with the intention of the Universe and helping it make good on its promise..."*
>
> -Michael Nitti

Notes -

Chapter 18 - *Calling Off the Search*

As you stand prepared to engage in the process of awarding yourself and others good trophies, there are still a few "things" you should know before you do…

First of all, now that you've discovered that you are inseparable from everything else, wouldn't it follow that your Good Trophy Room is likewise inseparable? And wouldn't this suggest that the room we've been calling *your* Good Trophy Room is, in fact, much more *universal* than that?

As always, all that you were able to see when you first stepped into this room was what you expected to see; your *personal* trophies in your *personal* trophy room – so that is what you saw. Yet this was simply an illusion born of your social conditioning, which at the same time prevented you from seeing anything you *didn't* expect to see. Consequently, as you break free of your conditioning, you will come to realize that this room is not as "personal" – nor as tiny – as you originally thought. Nor is it confined within your "local" mind.

In fact, *no one* has ever visited their "own" Good Trophy Room, as the perception that either trophy room is personal to *you* is simply an hallucination; one which you were quick to perceive just a few short chapters ago (when you were still "trapped" within your fishbowl). However, now that you know that this isn't *your* room, where do you suppose you'll be putting all your new trophies?

Well, you'll actually be storing them in the very same room. However, now that you've broken free of your social conditioning, you'll find it a lot more *crowded* than the last time you were in there. This time it's going to be full of trophies. *Zillions* of them. What's more, you'll no longer have to check in with the door guard before making a deposit, which is because his job was effectively eliminated the moment you broke free of your fishbowl!

Still, how is it that both your "perception of reality" and your Good Trophy Room got altered so dramatically in little more than the blink of an eye? Well, this is precisely how the universe shows up when perceived from a *transformed* perspective, which is how it is likely to continue to show up for you now that you've "fired" your door guard!

You see, "your" Good Trophy Room was *always* full. It's just that you couldn't see all the trophies because you were not expecting to see them from your socially-conditioned perspective – just as the natives were "unable" to see Columbus' ships in that harbor. Of course, it's not that they couldn't see them simply because they had never seen ships like that before (for many of us are exposed to things for the first time yet still perceive them within our consciousness), but because they had *no reason* to expect ships like that to exist. What's more, the lack of a reason didn't even show up as missing.

For example, if you don't *believe* that earning a million dollars a year is plausible (in other words, it's so beyond the realm of your existing reality that it doesn't even show up for you as something that should be considered), then you will <u>not</u> be open to seeing any avenues that could lead to you earning that kind of money – even if they do "show up in your harbor." As a matter of fact, this dynamic is *so* pervasive that you will actually be able to observe it occurring even *now* if you simply read the following verse out loud:

"There is nothing quite as beautiful
as Paris in the
the Spring"

So – how many times did you see the word "the"? If you are willing to admit it, you only saw it as many times as you were *expecting* to see it, which was <u>once</u>. And yet, the word "the" is actually included *twice.* Similarly, there was no reason for you to *expect* to see anything other than your "personal" trophies in either trophy room, which is why these are the only ones you ever saw!

Soon, however, we'll be re-visiting both of these rooms for the first time since you learned of your *oneness* with the universe, which means that you will now be able to see all of the trophies you didn't (or couldn't) see before. At least if you're *open* to seeing them.

Ultimately, what is available to each of us is the ability to "see things as they truly are" – rather than as perceived through inherited filters or conditioning. Undo your conditioning and you will see the truth. Retain your conditioning and you will see only what you expect to see – or will *not* see what you don't expect to see – as both "expecting" and "not expecting" are still expectations. Therefore, and in most cases, your life will play out pretty much *as expected.*

Given which, if your parent had a problem with alcohol, what might you expect? If your family or peers are not abundantly wealthy or if you're convinced that money doesn't grow on trees, what might you expect? Or, if the culture you were born into has not yet embraced the fact that "you are inseparable from the field of intelligence that creates the entire cosmos*," what might you expect?

Obviously, you should expect whatever you're expecting! In which case, can you see why it is so important to let go of your limiting expectations?

Fortunately, we do have the ability to let go of these limiting expectations because they are not innate, but exist solely as an outgrowth of our social and personal conditioning. In actuality, all of our limiting beliefs and expectations are born of our fear of not being good enough, which stems from the illusion that you and I are separate from everyone and everything else, including *Source.*

Therefore, as you are able to step beyond your conditioning and let go of this illusion, you will be empowered to re-connect with Source and to dissolve all of your limiting beliefs – at which point you will find that you have been blessed with unlimited access to both the "freedom of choice" and the ability to generate positive expectations!

*from the book: *"Power, Freedom, and Grace"* by Deepak Chopra

* * * * * * * * * * * * * * * * * * *

Coaching: In order to claim this freedom and ability for your self, it is important that you follow each segment of this equation in sequence; first you embrace your limiting expectations, then you let them go, and then you have choice. Most often, we resist accepting or embracing whatever we want to let go of, which dooms us from the start; which is because whenever you resist something, it will persist.

* * * * * * * * * * * * * * * * * * *

In the wake of embracing "this illusion" and letting go of your socially-conditioned expectations, can you see that the room we've been referring to as "your" Good Trophy Room is really nothing other than *the* Good Trophy Room? In fact, if we were to describe it more accurately, a more fitting name for it might be "the universal empowerment trophy room." Yet, let's simply refer to it as *The* Good Trophy Room from now on, shall we?

Still, if this really isn't *your* room, whose room is it? And if it's really home to a zillion trophies, to whom do they belong?

Quite simply, both this room and all the trophies belong to *no one* in particular and to *everyone* collectively (although you are more likely to recall the ones you placed in here yourself). In any case, no matter how many of them are "yours," all of us have been storing our personal trophies in this *universal* trophy room forever.

What's more, you are more than welcome to add to this collection at any time – for what is preventing you from awarding yourself or others good trophies whenever it serves you to do so? In fact, what is preventing anyone from awarding themselves or anyone else good trophies at will? Ah yes – *Social conditioning!*

Well, at least you're learning to appreciate life beyond the fishbowl. Yet, after having spent the last eighteen chapters exploring the extent to which social conditioning has affected you, is there any reason why you would withhold any of this from others? After all, if you were to encourage the people in your life to step beyond their conditioning (by either coaching them personally or by recommending this book), wouldn't that be worthy of both another trophy and a trip into the Good Trophy Room whenever you did so?

Of course it would. Yet there are plenty of other ways to earn your way in as well, which is because the only thing standing between you and this room is a *good trophy* – and it doesn't even have to be your own! In fact, once you embrace both the premise and the promise of the Good Trophy Room, you will discover that you have been blessed with unlimited access to all of the good in the universe, including the power to create it *at will* – which is because you have every ability to do something trophy-worthy whenever you choose.

Let this in! Imagine how remarkable life will show up once you have re-trained your mind to continually be on the lookout for incidents deserving of good trophies. Especially as opposed to how less-than-remarkable it's played out while you've been incessantly and unwittingly searching for proof that you aren't good enough.

Remember, you are the door guard! Thus, whenever you observe anyone (including yourself) acting intentionally and in alignment with the greater good (rather than from survival), you will be empowered to deposit a trophy in this room!

Surely, once you expect to see these things, you will – especially as you allow yourself to be moved and inspired by every deserving action you come to witness. Be it *courage* in the face of fear, *determination* in the face of despair, *compassion* in response to sadness, or *love* in appreciation of anything – or any other positive intention initiated in support of the greater good. Any time you notice any of these things – *it's trophy time!*

What's more, this would include anything worthy that may appear to have happened by accident, in that all of our blessing*s* are deserving of good trophies as well. After all, don't you and I plant the seeds from which all good fortune tends to blossom?

Given all this, let's take pause to consider a few of the zillion trophies *already* in this room. Can you see that you have access to some pretty powerful "stuff?" In fact, if you simply think on these things and *expect* to see them, you'll be able to associate to "all of the good" that was ever perpetuated by anyone upon anyone else.

Can you appreciate the enormity of this truth?

What this means is that if you are *willing* to see it, *you will.* Every time Mother Teresa held the hand of a dying orphan and allowed that child to feel the love of the Divine Spirit coming through her. Every time Jesus comforted a Leper. Every time Muhammad spoke of forgiveness. Every time the Buddha shared his wisdom. Every time Anne Frank wrote another page in her diary. Every time Gandhi or Martin Luther King took a stand for freedom. Every time a paramedic saves a life. Every time a father bounces his child on his knee, or every time a mother bathes her newborn and kisses it on the forehead. I promise you that all of this is in this room – plus countless other events that you are aware of either personally or historically. Yet, as you now know, these are all one and the same.

Who you are is "one" with every one of these events, meaning that you are inseparable from all of the good that has ever occurred (or has yet to occur)! If it happened in a moment of *Source* recognizing itself as *Source*, then it's in this room – and *you* have the ability to associate to all of it – and to be empowered by the love and magnificence of it all.

Allow yourself to be inspired by this. *Focus* on these things. Let them in. *This* is the power of the Good Trophy Room; to know that you contributed to it. To know that it is you who is contributing your love – *even at this moment* – as both you and Mother Teresa are surely holding that orphans hand as you read this. She will never let it go – and neither must you. But, if you should let it go, what part of *oneness* have you not yet embraced that would prevent you from experiencing yourself *as one* with Mother Teresa? You are *she* and she is *you.* Allow this in. And then "be" it. Close your eyes and *be* with her as she holds that orphans hand. Allow yourself to be moved. And then go give *that* to someone else. For *that* is who you are. And then give yourself a trophy.

Are you inspired yet? I have faith that you are – and that you'll bring this inspiration with you "across the hall" – as we're about to revisit *the* Bad Trophy Room for the first time since you left your fishbowl behind. And how many trophies do you suspect we'll see in there this time? That's right. *Zillions!*

Surely, you must be thinking, I'm mistaken – as this room is supposed to be closed. And, in fact, both of us know that you did "shut it down" just a few short chapters ago. Which is why, immediately after our visit, you'll be free to close it right back down if that is your desire. Yet, as you're about to discover, there's really no reason to do so...

As you'll recall, when you first stepped into this Trophy Room (before you knew of it as "bad" and back when you considered it *yours*), all that you were expecting to see were the trophies you put in here yourself. However, as you have since discovered, this room is actually home to <u>all</u> the bad trophies that have been awarded *by anyone* as proof that *no one* has ever been good enough. In other words, this room is filled with centuries-upon-centuries of proof that humanity, itself, is a threat to its own survival. In which case, my estimate of "zillions" may be a little bit *low...*

Whatever the estimate, there is no question that this room is home to a whole lot of evidence that we rarely treat each other as well as we could. Consequently, a whole lot of proof that human beings <u>react</u> a lot more often than not out of <u>survival</u> – which (as has been so clearly demonstrated throughout history), explains our need to dominate, to win, to be right, and to justify it all. As a result, there's a trophy in this room for every time one of us has responded to a threat in this manner. Meaning it's probably closer to *ten* zillion.

In any case, this room is overflowing with a multitude of things that most of us do not want to accept. And although this is certainly understandable, it is not at all in alignment with *the truth.* You see, the essence of our "inseparability" is that we are absolutely inseparable from everything else. Remember, you are *everything* and everything is *you* – including all of the "bad stuff" in this room. We do not get to pick and choose what we are "inseparable from," as that would be an inclination born inside the fishbowl.

As you are able to experience yourself as "one with everything," (hence, inseparable from *that* which is responsible for all of the bad trophies in this room), you will discover that you have no issue with any of these bad trophies – nor any attachment to what they represent. For they simply represent *what's so.*

Therefore, there is freedom to be had in recognizing everything in this room *without* prejudice or judgment; which would have been impossible from inside the fishbowl. After all, this room is overflowing with frustration, anger, upset, and blame – not to mention all of the oppression and injustice one can imagine – including every war, the holocaust, and "the whole of man's inhumanity to man." Every time a human being fell short or reacted out of fear, someone put a trophy in this room.

Given which, can you see that *this* is what you've actually been present to whenever you visited this room? Of course, you may not have seen all of these things as clearly as you saw all of your "own" trophies (primarily because you were not *expecting* to see them), yet how could you have not been affected by all the negative energy? Again, "the truth is the truth" whether you perceive it or not, so you likely felt all of this even if you only caught glimpses of it from time to time. What's more, all of these things are *still* in this room – and *always will be...*

Thus, it will serve you to acknowledge *the truth,* which is that although each of us has the ability to *not* revisit or focus on the content of this room, one can never cause it to disappear (which is because everything is *forever).* Therefore, I invite you to step beyond the need to experience the content of either trophy room as "good" or "bad" and to simply embrace it as *content.* For, as Shakespeare pointed out, *good* and *bad* are born exclusively of our thinking…

In fact, all of this "content" is inseparable from *Source,* which means that it *exists* as Source. Therefore, when you are *fully awake* you will experience *Source* in this content. In other words, on the other side of any consideration as to whether something is positive or negative – once you simply embrace it all – *God* shows up!

Remember, *everything* exists as pure consciousness, which is *forever.* Therefore, you can never shut down the "universal" Bad Trophy Room (nor the "universal *anything*" for that matter). In fact, there's no use in pretending that the Bad Trophy Room doesn't exist, for one cannot deny one room without denying the other. Instead, our most powerful option is to embrace all that we consider negative and take responsibility for it. We must grant it "beingness" and *include* it. Then, we can turn our thoughts to *love*…

"Your task is not to seek for love, but merely to seek and find all of the barriers within yourself that you have built against it."

-Rumi

Can you feel the love? If not, then you may still be standing in a little left over "water" from your fishbowl – because more often than not, the only thing that prevents us from *feeling* love is that we are *not expecting* to feel it.

In fact, love is omnipresent, so there's no need to go searching for it. It's a matter of acknowledging your*Self* as *Source* – hence, the *source* of love. You are not separate from love. It is *within* you. Bring it forth. Give it away. Most of us wait until someone else tells us that they love us before we say it back. You must not hold back. Love shows up in the expression of it. Yet most of us believe that we must first "feel" it *before* we can express it. Not so. It is a simultaneous creation – yet must be initiated from an intention to do so. This is why love so often shows up as scarce, because most of us are *waiting* for it to show up. Quit waiting. If everyone is waiting, then who is going to go first? In celebration of that which is in *me*, which is also in *you*, I invite you to *go first.*

Love is not a commodity. It is not in short supply. You will not run out. Therefore, let it flow freely as the fullest expression of your *Self.* As *divine energy* flows through you, so does love. Hence, we not only make love happen, we *allow* it to happen. By "creating it" as it flows through us. You must stop resisting! And what is it to "stop resisting" other than "letting go"? Therefore, let go! Let it *all* go – all of your strongly held beliefs, all of your righteousness, and all of your resentments.

When you do, all that will be left is *love*...

Ultimately, give it *all* up – including all of your reasons for not giving it up. It's time. Live in the stillness of the truth. Live as the whole and complete being that you are. After all, the fact that you are whole and complete is true whether you choose to align with it or not, so why not align? In fact, the ability to live intentionally, freely, gracefully, gratefully, and lovingly is nothing more than the willingness to honor *that,* which is already present. There is no need to go searching for anything.

Therefore, call off the search! At least the search for anything *outside* yourself. If you are looking for something outside yourself to "complete" you, then you are looking for external objects, which come and go. In fact, even the search for good trophies requires that you look outside yourself for something that you have told yourself you don't already have – which is futile.

Does this mean I'm suggesting that you call off the search for good trophies??

As a matter of fact, I am. But not before you're able to perceive their existence without having to search for them. You see, you will not need to go "searching" for good trophies once you're able to experience yourself and others as whole and complete in every moment – and able to acknowledge the "already existence" of any and all good trophies without conducting a search. In fact, you won't require proof of your oneness with anything once you experience yourself in this manner and then trust your experience.

Again, the Good Trophy Room is already full. It always was. In fact, you are already "one" with all the good trophies in this room.

Thus, I invite you to choose to align with the love that you are – as well as the power, freedom, and harmony that you already possess. In this regard, you are not so much searching for good trophies, as you are simply acknowledging their "already-ness." In other words, you are *honoring* them rather than *searching* for them. As such, even when you consciously and intentionally award or accept a new trophy, the experience is one of appreciating it and being grateful for it – not so much as a *new* discovery, but more as if visiting an *old friend* – one whom you enjoy meeting as often as possible because it "fills you up" and enlivens you to do so.

What is available as a result of acknowledging your *Self* in this manner is nothing less than a complete transformation of your sense of being in the world; a shift from "wondering" to *knowing.* A "knowing" that you are in charge of both your psychology and your destiny because *The Trophy Effect* is now on your side.

Just like an old friend.

However, until you find yourself revisiting all of your good trophies "as old friends" on a more consistent basis, the most effective way to re-condition your behavior is to actively and intentionally award good trophies to both yourself and others as often as you possibly can!

In support of making this a reality, the Exercises in the following chapter have been designed to both teach you how to do so and to keep you on track. Then, once you've settled into a routine of consistently recognizing all of the positive things in your life with good trophies, you'll eventually be able to "take the training wheels off." At which point, it's all downhill from there.

On the other hand, once you discover how much fun you are having and how magnificent you feel while doing these Exercises, you may just decide to leave the training wheels on. *Forever…*

"When you realize there is nothing lacking,
the whole world belongs to you."

–Lao Tzu

Coaching: Please be reminded that the purpose of the Exercises is to not only experience yourself as fully worthy and fully connected to your fellow human beings, but to overcome the innate fears that have separated you from the life you deserve. To this end, you will be encouraged to step willingly beyond where you normally stop with yourself and others. In order to insure your success, I suggest that you build this muscle slowly by accumulating as many small wins as possible before allowing the resultant momentum to stretch you further each day. By engaging in this manner, you should find that you are pushing "way past itsy-bitsy" by the middle of the third Exercise. Therefore, although you may "start small," do not stay small. Engage fully by both keeping your word to yourself and by empowering others. Stretch yourself - and have fun!

"He who tastes, knows"

-Sufi aphorism

Chapter 19 - *The Exercises; Unlearning the Past and Enlarging the Future*

"You, yourself, as much as anybody in the universe, deserve your love and affection."

-Buddha

Well, I see you're still here, so you obviously "survived" the last chapter. In which case, congratulations! But this time, can you see it was the *Self* who pulled you through and not your mind? Therefore, please give your Self a trophy.

And, if you feel like you've at least begun to grasp what was revealed in the last three chapters, give yourself another trophy. A big one.

Again, even if you're still attempting to make sense of it all, I acknowledge both your intention and your perseverance – so please award yourself a trophy in honor of that. After all, given that you've been *socially conditioned* to see things other than how they really are, it wouldn't at all be unusual for you to find yourself bouncing back and forth between "seeing it" and "not seeing it" or "grasping it" and "not grasping it" – at least until you *get it* for good!

Frankly, back when I was initially exposed to the true nature of things, I clearly recall bumping up against my own social conditioning for quite some time. For although I had an immediate sense that what my teachers were pointing at was true, I remember it being quite a struggle for me to let go of my fishbowl.

Fortunately, I was eventually coached through a similar series of exercises that prompted me to play full out in spite of my fears until I finally "got it for good" – at which point, I spontaneously broke free of my fishbowl. In light of which, here's a little coaching on how to approach these Exercises: *play full out!!!*

The bottom line is that if you allow what you've learned about *The Trophy Effect* to inspire you and then take the Exercises to heart, you are bound to experience a major shift in how you feel about yourself and others within as little as a few short weeks – especially compared to how you felt before you read this book and did the Exercises. In fact, you are practically guaranteed a breakthrough if you simply follow through. However, if you truly play full out, what is available is a *whole lot more* than that.

So, are you beginning to appreciate that the best way to get the result is to do the Exercises?

Again, the primary objective of these Exercises is not happiness. But, if they did make you happy, would that be okay? I hope so. You deserve to be happy.

Still (and although I predict that happiness will show up fairly soon), the primary intent of these Exercises is to re-condition your mind to "be on the lookout" for evidence of your worthiness rather than proof that you aren't good enough (while at the same time establishing new neural-pathways within your brain that lead directly into the Good Trophy Room). Hence, the *ultimate* outcome is to "undo" your social conditioning and to replace it with the ability to see things as they *really* are.

In support of making this happen, I encourage you to engage as fully as possible with each of the following Exercises, which have been designed to evoke a shift in your psychology from "unconscious to *conscious*" and from "reactionary to *intentional.*" In other words, these Exercises are intended to cause you to think and act *on purpose!*

As you are about to discover, the very act of engaging with these Exercises will cause you to align with this intention, thereby allowing you to access your natural state of "Being" – a state from which you will be able to experience yourself as one with Source. At which point, you will discover that you are able to "see" Divine Energy (Source / God) in everything…

You and I are the creators of our lives. Yet, in the absence of perceiving ourselves in this manner, most of us have been reduced to "hoping" that it will all work out. However, when one is committed to living *intentionally* and *on purpose,* there is no need for hope. What's more, once you give up "waiting to be saved" by something outside yourself, you will no longer be left to wonder whether life will turn out. Therefore, I invite you to align with that part of you which *is* the creator, as it is from this perspective that you will ultimately come to realize that you don't need saving!

"The world rewards those who take responsibility for their own success."

-Curt Gerrish

This, then, is where the Exercises come in – as they will support you in taking actions that are consistent with *being* the creator of your life. Even if you are unable to recognize this or "feel it" all at once, so long as you *act* like you are the creator (by *doing* the exercises), your brain will begin to generate new neural-pathways and your mind will eventually align with what you are doing. Therefore, by simply incorporating these Exercises into your daily routine, your limiting beliefs will soon be replaced with the "knowing" that you truly are the author of your own experience!

Of course, as is true with everything else in life, the more you put into this, the more you'll get out of it. So I invite you to follow the instructions as best you can – *and have fun!!*

"We first make our habits and then our habits make us."

-John Dryden

Note: The following four Exercises should be *initiated* in order, however, you may begin the 2nd Exercise before completing the 1st, and the 3rd Exercise before completing the 2nd. However, please do not begin the 4th Exercise until you have completed the first three.

Exercise # 1: ***Award yourself good trophies from your past.***

What you'll need: A journal or a notebook, to be entitled "The Good Trophy Room (a custom Workbook is available and may be downloaded, free of charge, at www.thetrophyeffect.com).

The purpose of this Exercise is to identify the numerous positive experiences in your life that never made it past your door guard and into the Good Trophy Room. Thus, your assignment is to finally award yourself *good trophies* for all the worthy incidents in your past that you previously failed to recognize with trophies (a process that will begin to re-condition your behavior via the creation of new neural-pathways within your brain).

First, however, it is very important that you:

1) Give up any notion you may have that good trophies are "special and rare" or any aversion you may have to patting yourself (or anyone else) on the back.
2) Be open to modifying your "evaluation criteria" in recognition of the fact that you are *already* worthy and magnificent; thus, fully able to award and receive good trophies.

As you know, your old rating system was invented in the fishbowl, so *let it go...*

To begin, allow at least 45 minutes for the "reflect & capture" portion of this Exercise, taking additional time (as needed) to capture all that you are able; continuing to add new things to the list as you recall them over the next few days. Also, there is no need to record things chronologically, so if your memory of a specific situation when you were *seven* prompts you to recall a similar situation when you were *twenty-seven,* simply make note of them as you remember them. Again, you are re-visiting these incidents in order to acknowledge the presence of "good intention" and to appreciate your worthiness where you hadn't done so before…

For my fifth birthday, my parents threw me a party – yet the memory lived inside my Bad Trophy Room as proof that I wasn't good enough for 25 years. During that party, my mother deliberately took a toy from me and gave it to a friend with whom I'd been fighting – at which point (although I certainly didn't know it at the time), I awarded myself a very large bad trophy. I felt unworthy and betrayed and started to cry – so I also felt embarrassed. In that moment, I was instantaneously transported into the Bad Trophy Room, where I recall making several life-shaping decisions: I wasn't good enough, my mother wasn't good enough, friends cannot be trusted, birthday parties are overrated, etc. In fact, for much of my life, I refused to allow anyone to throw me a party or otherwise make a big deal of my birthday – yet I *believed* it was because I was being humble.

Upon freeing myself from my fishbowl, I was able to re-evaluate this incident from a *transformed perspective* – at which point, I replaced the bad trophy I had originally earned with several good ones. I realized that I was being selfish with my toys and that my mother was simply trying to teach me a valuable lesson about sharing. It was as simple as that. Thus, I also did away with the bad trophy that I had given her for being mean and uncaring (you never made a decision like this about either of *your* parents, did you?) and gave her a good trophy instead. On top of that, I realized that I was worthy and deserved the birthday party – and recalled getting lots of nice presents from lots of great friends! I also saw that I was human. In light of all this, I gave myself about six good trophies!

In fact, most of us have memories of similar incidents, so if you are able to identify one and "turn it around," please do. However, the primary intent of this Exercise is to identify specific situations when "good things" happened (including times when you did things for others or when others did things for you), yet your social conditioning and the fear of not being good enough prevented you from experiencing those incidents as deserving of a trophy.

Again, the outcome is to teach you how to override your "default conditioning" by having you re-evaluate incidents that you failed to appreciate at the time they occurred. I assure you that your past is sprinkled with a multitude of worthy events that you didn't value as such only because they were perceived through the filter of your inherited conditioning. This Exercise will not only permit you to "re-invent" and appreciate your *past,* but will enable you to perceive your *future* from a far less critical (and more empowering) perspective!

> *Reminder; you and I are fully capable of experiencing ourselves as both magnificent and humble at the same time, so please be willing to let go of any resistance you may have to completing this Exercise.*

If you're a mother, although you likely believe that you could have done better, how many times have you nursed tiny wounds, consoled hurt feelings, served a favorite meal, or read a bedtime story? If you're not a mother, have you ever done any of these things as an aunt or a big sister? If you're a father (or ever assumed this role for any reason), although you may also think that you could have done better, there are undoubtedly many good things that you have done either *with* or *for* your children – so please be sure to award yourself all the trophies you deserve...

Speaking of parents, please allow yourself to recall anything supportive that your mother or father may have done for you – even if you're convinced that one or both of them fell short – and capture all of these things in your journal. And, if you'd be willing to "take away" any *bad* trophies you ever awarded either of them, now would be the perfect time to give yourself a *good* trophy for doing so.

Otherwise, have you ever thrown anyone a party? Sent anyone a greeting card? Given anyone a gift? Come on, how many times have you picked up a restaurant tab, bought someone a cup of coffee, or treated a friend to ice cream? Write all of these things down and enjoy thinking about all this stuff! Think about all of the times you treated *anyone* to *anything* and recall the moment of pleasure you caused. No matter how small. Then, think back on those situations when someone did the same for you and give them a trophy as well. *Hint: old photos, scrapbooks, or year-books often come in handy in support of this exercise.*

Can you play a musical instrument? Did you ever excel in a sport? Have you ever made the Honor Roll (or done relatively well in spite of some disadvantage)? Keep thinking! Have you ever cleaned your house? Yes, a good house cleaning deserves a trophy! Do not allow your old *fishbowl conditioning* to turn this into a struggle. In fact, although you must be sure to include the "small stuff," it may serve you to begin with "the biggies" just to get the juices flowing. In which case, if you paid for anyone's surgery or for any weddings, please be sure to add these to your list. And, speaking of getting the juices flowing, many of our fondest memories have to do with sex and intimacy – so don't forget to acknowledge any memorable sexual experiences. Even if this subject has caused you pain at times, do not rob yourself of honoring those moments when you shared yourself lovingly with another human being.

Next, include anything that others have done for you, as well as anything you've observed others doing for others (which could easily cause your list to triple in size). The bottom line is that if something occurred as the result of *good intention* and within range of your awareness – and you did not previously honor it with a good trophy – now is the time to do so by capturing it in your journal!

Finally, continue with this Exercise until you have at least *200* entries. But don't be shy about capturing more than that! I've worked with clients who kept writing over the course of several days until they filled much of their journal – at which point, their lives were magically transformed. So, why would you stop? Yet, you likely will stop short of capturing the thousands of incidents you could recall if you didn't stop, for at some point I predict that you will simply surrender into the truth of your worthiness and come to realize that you possess far more autonomy over your perceptions and expectations than you ever imagined!

In support of this, please review your journal entries as often as possible over the course of the next two weeks, allowing yourself to be empowered by this truer and happier version of your past – and make note of any additional insights you may have as a result of doing this Exercise.

"What a wonderful life I've had!
I only wished I'd realized it sooner."

-Colette

Exercise # 2: *Consciously bring forth and acknowledge good intention and recognize every positive incident with a good trophy.*

What you'll need: a) The same journal used in Exercise #1, yet this will be an ongoing process, so reserve plenty of blank pages, or b) A small notepad in case you prefer not to carry your journal with you, as you'll be making notes throughout the day.

The purpose of this Exercise is to train your-Self to be on the lookout for any and all expressions of good intention and to identify any situation where you (or others) have acted intentionally in the face of any fear or inclination not to. As you know, our fear of not being good enough is innate, so the most effective way to counter this fear is to acknowledge the truth of our collective magnificence by awarding lots of trophies (which will create another *positive* neural-connection within your brain every time you do).

Once you are fully present to the fact that we are all "whole and complete with nothing lacking," the fear of not being good enough has no power over you.

Therefore, I encourage you to immerse yourself in this Exercise until you find that you are consistently looking for evidence that you are worthy rather than proof that you are not. To which end, it will serve you to continue collecting evidence (awarding trophies) until you have constructed this *new* reality over top of your *old* reality. Thereby causing fear to take a permanent back seat to the truth!

"You never change things by fighting the existing reality. To change something, build a new model that makes the old model obsolete."

-Buckminster Fuller

In support of this outcome, it is critical that you keep your eyes peeled for every little thing that is deserving of a trophy – and then make note of it in your journal. As with the first Exercise, this will require that you give up any notion that good trophies are "special and rare," as well as any aversion you may have to patting yourself (or anyone else) on the back.

Again, once you begin looking for "good things," you *will* see them. Allow yourself to be moved and inspired by every act of positive intention you come to observe. Be it courage, determination, empathy, compassion, encouragement, excellence, contribution, or love – or any other evidence that the universe is unfolding as an expression of *Source.* Any time you witness any of these things, *it's trophy time!*

Recently, I was in a grocery store waiting to check out when I noticed two women in line at the next register. Both had children in tow and were attempting to unload their groceries onto the conveyer while keeping an eye on the kids. I could tell that the one lady had observed something about the woman in front of her that had prompted her to chuckle – and I could see that she was about to say something but didn't. I watched as she began to speak and then stopped short, which she did *several* times before finally excusing herself to say what she wanted to say. Evidently, whatever she said was well received because the other woman laughed and responded in kind, at which point there existed an immediate rapport – a *connection* – and within seconds they were both chatting away, which prompted the lady who had just finished checking out to wait for her "new friend" at the door. I continued to watch as they kept laughing all the way into the parking lot, where they finally parted ways with giant smiles on their faces.

First of all, if I hadn't been open to seeing this little interaction, I wouldn't have noticed it, yet what would I have missed? Was this really such a big deal?

Well, what I saw was *the truth.* I had observed a human being who had allowed herself to be moved by another – who then struggled with her *fear of not being good enough* before finally speaking. I witnessed a tug-of-war between the Self and the mind where the Self ultimately won, at which point the one lady acted with an intention to empower the other. She had brought forth empathy. I then observed the other lady reciprocate by allowing herself to be moved, rather than simply dismiss the act with a "thank you" and hurry to her car, which I noticed she was about to do before she reconsidered and decided to wait; hence, another intentional act on the other side of a tug-of-war, that was won by the *Self.* I then got to watch two fully present and empowered human beings laugh their way into the parking lot, as their kids were becoming fast friends as well – more likely than not because they were empowered by *the joy of aliveness* that existed between the two mothers.

In any case, because I allowed myself to be empowered by this whole interaction, all three of us got trophies – and I returned to my car a lot more inspired than when I arrived at the store – which inspired me to go to the beach to be with nature for a while. All because a stranger pushed through her fears and said something she could have just as easily withheld. She could have lost that tug-of-war and I'd have likely gone straight home without awarding anyone any trophies.

In support of you being able to replicate this Exercise, please make note of a few things about this incident: it happened in a public place, it involved people I didn't know, and it had nothing to do with me – and it would have gone unnoticed had I not been *looking* for it.

Although what I observed inside the store was relatively subtle, on the way out of the grocery store, I paused to buy a box of Girl Scout cookies (also taking time to commend the salesmanship of the young lady who was selling them) and then helped a woman lift a heavy case of bottled water from the bottom of her shopping cart into her trunk. Bingo! Two more trophies. Pretty easy, huh?

Yes, it *is* easy once you are looking for situations such as these, but please be clear that this Exercise is not about doing "good deeds" (although what would be so terrible about that?). It's about empowerment and aligning with intention *(Source).*

What's important to notice is that I did not have to go out of my way to make any of these things happen because each one of these opportunities presented itself – and was accomplished – within the context of my daily routine. However, if I hadn't trained myself to be on the lookout for trophy-worthy situations, then what may I have observed in each case?

Well, I might have seen two mothers who weren't able to prevent their bratty kids from disturbing other customers, *or* I could have been annoyed by the cookie stand blocking the exit in order to shame me into buying cookies, *or* I could have seen a lady who was too meek to ask the clerk for assistance to her car. But I didn't. I saw what I saw, *and so can you...*

As you continue to make note of the dozens of trophy-worthy incidents that occur each day, remember to capture *all* of them in your journal – which will serve as your "temporary" trophy room until you condition your mind to capture and retain these incidents on its own. In this regard, the same dynamic will occur on paper as it does in the Good Trophy Room, which is because every time you make an addition to the list, you will be prompted to notice all of the good things *already* on the list. In fact, I invite you to bring as much enjoyment to this process as possible – perhaps by employing a fine leather journal, using colored pens, or by writing in random locations on the pages – much like you would if autographing a yearbook. You're in charge, so make it *fun.*

While fun is a good thing, your first priority must be to capture your "trophy-earning moments" as they occur. Therefore, although you are certainly welcome to employ an existing PDA or a day planner, what may serve you best is a simple pocket notepad. Still, even if you simply write things down on "post-its," you must remember to transfer everything into your primary journal at least once per day (which will provide you with yet another opportunity to feel good about these things as you do). In any case, it's essential that you "anchor in" all of your good trophies by *writing them down.*

As important as this may be, it's your newly-modified "rules and guidelines" that are vital to your success. Therefore, it's imperative that you make it as easy as possible to award yourself good trophies. In other words, *lighten up!* This is *your* life. You get to invent the rules. If you choose to acknowledge yourself for making your bed, what a marvelous way to start the day!

In fact, no matter how you begin your day, if you do so by keeping your word to yourself, that's a trophy! Did you work out? Did you prepare anyone a nice breakfast (including yourself)? With whom in your family did you share some love before going your separate ways? Whatever you do, there are surely several trophies "waiting to happen" somewhere within your morning routine.

Do you drive to work? If so, would you be willing to allow another driver to cut in front of you where you typically would have sped up to prevent that from happening? Or, perhaps, someone else let you go first. Either way, it's trophy time!

As you can see, you could easily collect a dozen trophies before you even reach your workplace (however, please don't capture them while driving). In fact, it may serve you to pause several times each day to think back on what's happened up to that point in order to record anything you may have overlooked – including anything worthy that "seems" to have happened by accident.

Allow yourself to be moved and inspired by every *act of intention* you observe. Whether it's you doing something in support of someone else or somebody else doing something for you – or *anyone* doing *anything* in support of another (including incidents as subtle as the ones I witnessed at the grocery store). No matter how trivial an incident may seem, if it was born of a positive intention, please apply your newly revised rules and guidelines and honor it with a trophy.

* * * * * * * * * * * * * * * * * * *

Additional examples of "positive intention"; *holding a door for a stranger, allowing someone to go ahead of you in a check check-out line, acknowledging a brilliant performance at an entertainment event, sending or receiving a thank-you card or email, leaving a generous tip, taking out a neighbors trash, or simply offering someone an intentional, loving smile.*

* * * * * * * * * * * * * * * * * * *

As you can imagine, if you truly play full out, you will either initiate or encounter dozens of trophy-worthy incidents every day, which means that you'll likely be pausing fairly often to make notes in your journal. However, if you are a "Type A" personality or are otherwise resistant to taking notes, you may notice a little reluctance with regard to this Exercise. If so, can you see that the very act of *pushing through* your resistance in order to capture things in writing would be deserving of a trophy? After all, isn't "pushing through" an intentional act?

Therefore – and no matter whether you're "Type A" or not, please be willing to cause such a breakthrough by taking a moment to record your trophies in writing, while giving yourself an *addi-*

tional "pat on the back" every time you do; which will also cause the creation of another *neural connection* within your brain.

In any case, whether you choose to employ a journal, a notepad, or your PDA (or simply scribble your trophy on a scrap piece of paper), please transfer as much of what you capture each day into your Good Trophy Room journal each night.

Once you've mastered this process, I invite you to continue this Exercise for at least two more weeks – or until you are certain that you have fully conditioned yourself to "perceive your world" in this manner. In support of which, please review your journal at least once per day, allowing yourself to be empowered by your ever-expanding sense of intentionality and worthiness!

"Increasing your self-esteem is easy. Simply do good things and remember that you did them."
–John Roger

Exercise # 3: ***Consciously bring forth an intention to express your magnificence as often as possible and then award yourself good trophies when you do so.***

What you'll need: Same as Exercise #2

The purpose of this Exercise is to demonstrate your ability to express your intention *at will,* thereby proving to yourself that you have full power over your focus and your actions. What is available is the experience of being fully responsible for your own life (thus, the experience of yourself as *the creator* of your life), as demonstrated by your ability to *act intentionally* whenever you choose.

We have been blessed with the power of choice and the ability to manifest our own destiny, yet most of us remain impotent in the face of our social conditioning and our fears. As a result, our lives are often filled with drama and distractions that prevent us from experiencing our *oneness with Source* – thereby impeding the natural flow of intention and love. This Exercise will enable you to breakthrough all of this, allowing you access to this natural flow of *Divine energy.*

In Exercise #2 your mission was to acknowledge the trophy-worthy situations you encountered on a daily basis without having to go too far out of your way. In this Exercise, the bar has been raised – meaning that you will soon be presented with the opportunity to earn some very special trophies by venturing *beyond* your fishbowl. Therefore, I invite you to play full out in order to discover what is available on the other side of doing so.

"Everything you want is just outside your comfort zone."

-Robert Allen

In the previous Exercise, an example of "not having to go too far out of your way" may have been helping someone load groceries into their car, which was parked directly next to your own. In that situation, although your action was fully deserving of a trophy, the opportunity more or less presented itself to you. In this Exercise, an example of "stepping beyond your fishbowl" would be to notice someone in similar need of help *on the other side of the parking lot* (which would definitely require that you go out of your way) and then, after joyfully lending a hand, returning their shopping cart to the store.

Your mission is to be on the lookout for situations that require you to stretch yourself beyond the norm. Situations where your mind whispers into your ear that you're going too far or that you're about to look foolish and then implores you to quit. Instead, this is precisely when you'll know that you're on the right track, as the outcome of this Exercise is to discover what happens when you *intentionally override your mind* in favor of doing something you normally wouldn't do.

Still, this Exercise is not about doing "good deeds" – but that's precisely what you would be doing if you simply helped someone with their groceries and then went about your day. In which case, you may be deserving of a *merit badge* but not a trophy.

Remember, this time we've raised the bar. The only way to earn a good trophy during this Exercise is by truly *connecting* with someone. Again, this isn't about playing "good deed tag" – whereby you sneak in, collect a trophy, and be on your way. Instead, you must establish and complete a "cycle of connection" – a situation where two human beings have understood that a difference was made and acknowledged their *oneness* in that moment. For instance, when delivering a compliment or lending someone a hand, you must elicit a response. Make sure that it's acknowledged (even if it's just a smile) and then acknowledge that back. Once you experience this, you may award yourself a trophy.

One fairly extreme, yet otherwise perfect, example of this occurred when one of my long-time clients encountered an elderly gentleman with a walker who was entering a public restroom as my client was leaving. At first, he simply held the door but then realized that the gentleman was in need of additional help, as he was shaking visibly and seemed to be having trouble maneuvering his way inside. In support, my client steadied the walker and guided the gentleman by the elbow while walking him *s-l-o-w-l-y* to the urinal.

At this point, my client's mind was whispering into his ear that holding the door would have been sufficient and to leave while the leaving was good – but instead, he asked the gentleman, "Are you okay?" To which the man responded "No." By this time, my clients mind was no longer whispering, but *imploring* him to leave without asking any more foolish questions. However, my client refused to listen to his mind and instead inquired as to what was wrong. "I can't get my zipper down," the man replied.

By then, my client's mind was literally *screaming* at him to wish the man well and to leave at once – yet, my client pushed through his "discomfort" and proceeded to help the gentleman with his zipper.

However, for whatever reason – perhaps because he was already nervous – the man was suddenly shaking so badly that he reported he could not *free himself* from his pants to do what he came to do. And just who do you suppose helped "free him" from his pants?

What happened that day is that my client walked into that restroom as the person *he wasn't* and walked out of it as the person *he was.* He had been transformed. And although he didn't know *how* it happened, what he did know was that for one brief, beautiful moment, his mind actually *shut up.* It went silent. In the end, he did not have to push past his mind, because it literally disappeared when the *Self* showed up. And when the Self showed up, so did courage, empathy, compassion, and love.

So, does this mean that in order to play full out you're going to have to hang out in public restrooms? Of course not. Yet you must be willing to step into situations where you are prepared to keep telling your mind to shut up – *until it does.*

No matter what, keep putting yourself out there. Remain on the lookout for situations where you can make a difference – and then speak and act with the intention to leave another human being more empowered than they were before you showed up. Again, this Exercise is not about slipping into a situation, doing a good deed, and then slipping out with a trophy. It's about pushing *beyond* where you normally stop with yourself and others.

Even so, this entire process of awarding trophies is not about "making you better." You are *already* better. It is about being intentional, experiencing your connectedness, and empowering others to feel the same. Therefore, as you play full out, please do so with the intention of breaking through rather than in an attempt to prove to the universe that you are capable of playing full out. You are *already* capable. Of course, on the other side of pushing beyond your fears, it's entirely probable that you will feel even better and more capable than you have in years. In fact, it's very likely that you will feel as happy as you've ever felt before – yet this is simply a pleasant *side effect,* rather than an outcome of this Exercise…

Therefore, even if it makes you happy, I invite you to remain on the look-out for situations where you will be required to step beyond your comfort zone, such as:

1) Gladly going beyond the call of duty
2) Adding significantly more value than another would expect
3) Doing something for someone so that they don't have to
4) Giving someone the gift of your listening and your empathy
5) Practice excellence by pushing beyond "good enough"
6) Offering an honest and empowering acknowledgement
7) Re-establishing a relationship by resolving an "incompletion" or misunderstanding from the past

In fact, why not intend to do all of these things – and *more* – as often as possible over the course of the next few weeks?

As with Exercise #2, please capture these incidents as they occur either in your notebook or by whatever means you've chosen – and then transfer whatever you capture each day into your Good Trophy Room journal each night. Also, make note of any insights you may have as a result of doing this Exercise.

Finally, I invite you to continue this process for at least two weeks – or until you feel that you've truly experienced a breakthrough or have otherwise achieved the outcome. Until then, please review your journal as often as possible, allowing yourself to be empowered by your ever-expanding experience of *Self* and your connectedness with others.

"By becoming a conscious choice-maker, you begin to generate actions that are evolutionary for you."

-Deepak Chopra

Exercise # 4: *Gratefulness (Loving "what's so")*
& Forgiveness (Getting to "so what")

What you'll need: Your Good Trophy Room journal and a highlighter pen.

The purpose of this Exercise is to encourage you to spend as much time as possible in the Good Trophy Room with the dual outcome of expanding your sense of gratitude and fostering your willingness to forgive and let go.

As you know, the only way you've been able to gain access to the Good Trophy Room until now has been to earn your way in by identifying a worthy incident and showing the associated trophy to the door guard. However, in light of your recent discovery that you *are* the door guard (and always have been), can you see that you have (and always have had) the ability to wander in and out of this room whenever you want? In fact, are you beginning to "get" that you have the power to do just about *anything* you used to think you couldn't or shouldn't do?

After all, whose life are you living? If you choose to never go back into the Bad Trophy Room, who can force you? If you choose to award yourself a good trophy for washing your car or for clearing all of your emails, who says you can't? And, if you choose to walk right past the door guard (which is you) and into the Good Trophy Room without a trophy, who's going to stop you? In fact, who, other than you, is in charge of anything that has to do with any decision you will ever have to make? You got it. *No one.* It's all up to *you.*

In which case, what's preventing you from spending as much time as you want inside the Good Trophy Room? That's right. *Nothing.*

Therefore, let's begin by spending some quality time in this room feeling ***<u>Grateful</u>***:

First, plan some alone time and set aside at least 45 minutes for this portion of the exercise. Begin by re-reading and reviewing all of the entries from each of the first three exercises, highlighting any for which you are especially grateful.

Next, visualize yourself slipping past the "door guard" and into The Good Trophy Room, which is now filled with *everything* you just reviewed in your journal.

Then, begin to reflect upon a few of your newest trophies from each exercise – and then begin to expand your awareness in order to become fully conscious of as many good trophies as you can. In fact, allow yourself to close your eyes for periods of time throughout this process to better associate to these trophies.

Now, allow yourself to begin to focus on any specific trophies for which you are *especially* grateful. Trophies that represent gifts you were given or gifts you gave others – or times when you were overwhelmed by the love or appreciation for another human being. Continue to focus on being grateful and allow yourself to gravitate to whatever trophies may be revealed, at which point make note of them in your journal (under ***"Gratefulness")***, even if they're already highlighted.

Focus primarily on these specific trophies, yet be open to others slipping into your consciousness as well – and then allow yourself to be moved by the degree to which you've been blessed for all that you have and who you are – including the opportunity to engage in this exercise itself.

Surrender into this feeling of gratefulness and then focus on this for as long as it serves you to do so – and then, award yourself a special trophy for feeling grateful and put it on its own pedestal in the center of the Good Trophy Room.

Repeat this process as it serves you to do so – and record in your journal any insights you may have as a result of this process.

"Being grateful. That's the first step on the path to joy."
-Sarah Ban Breathnach

The second part of this Exercise is about *letting go.* It's about ***Forgiveness.***

This Exercise is about acknowledging your power as *the creator* of your life, thus your ability *to choose* to break free of anything you're holding onto – whenever you want to.

Most likely, any incident you've been unwilling or unable to forgive has lived as a "biggie" inside the Bad Trophy Room – thus, you may want to explore whether or not your decision to detach from this room hasn't already softened your anger or resentment to some degree.

Whether or not you already feel such a shift, it will serve you to re-evaluate any incident you haven't yet forgiven from *where you are now* versus *where you were* when the incident occurred. Frankly, unless you were "wronged" while reading this book, every incident you've been unwilling to let go of occurred *before* you became fully aware of *The Trophy Effect,* thus any and all decisions regarding this incident – including your beliefs about it – were made *inside* the Bad Trophy Room.

Obviously, if you suffered any form of abuse or were disrespected in any way, there is no way to justify this type of behavior. Yet, what is available when evaluating anything from this side of *The Trophy Effect* is the ability to segregate "the truth" from *the story* you've likely been telling yourself, especially with regard to *your* role in that story.

"Forgiveness in no way justifies the actions that caused your wounding, nor does it mean you have to seek out those who harmed you. It is simply a movement to release and ease your heart of the pain and hatred that binds it. It is the

harvested fruit of a season of darkness, followed by a season of growth and of very hard work."

-Dawna Markova

Therefore, the first step in forgiving anyone for anything is to re-evaluate the situation from your newly transformed point-of-view. You see, whatever happened that caused you to withhold your forgiveness occurred when you were still observing things from *inside* your fishbowl; back when you were continually looking for proof that you weren't good enough.

In almost all cases, any unwillingness or inability to let go or *forgive* is caused by the feeling that one isn't worthy of being forgiven themselves (i.e., not being good enough), hence the unwillingness to forgive whomever was at cause in the first place. However, once you come to know yourself as whole and complete *and fully worthy,* there is no reason to hold onto anything that proves otherwise.

Thus, the purpose of this Exercise is to re-evaluate any incident where you've been unwilling or unable to forgive someone for causing you pain or sorrow, with the intention of discovering *the truth*. And, as we all know, the truth shall set you free…

"Hate is a monkey on your back. It weighs you down. Hate may be destroying your life. Meanwhile, the person you hate may not know or care. He or she may even be dead. Forgiving is a gift to yourself. You forgive so you can get on with your life."

-Ron Potter Effron

To begin, please create the following heading in your journal: ***To be Forgiven***. I also recommend that you do this process immediately after completing the *gratefulness* portion of this Exercise. So please review the results of that process prior to proceeding...

First, identify any incidents you've been unable to forgive by writing down the name of the individual and a brief description of what happened.

Next, reflect upon each incident, one at a time, with the intent to determine when during the incident you decided *you weren't good enough.* Remember, this is an *innate fear* – thus, even when victimized by another, most of us tend to believe that if only we had been good enough, the incident wouldn't have occurred.

Notice that this incident delivered you directly into the Bad Trophy Room where you then made *several* decisions regarding this incident (do you recall the story about my 5th birthday) Whom did you blame for this incident? What other decisions did you make? Notice that you had no control over these decisions.

In situations where you may have been abused or suffered a major indignity, in addition to the perpetrator, did you blame *yourself* or anyone else? If so, who?

Now, disassociate from this incident as best you can and once more assume the identity of an unbiased consultant. From this perspective, think back on this incident and notice whether the perpetrator was attempting *to dominate* anyone else or to avoid the domination of their life in general. Did they do what they did in order *to win,* to *be right,* or to prove that they were good enough because they were concerned that they were not? In other words – and although this does not justify their actions – did the perpetrator act or react out of *survival?*

Continuing to observe this incident as a consultant, can you see that the victim (you) had no choice but to make the decisions they made or to feel how they've felt ever since? Can you now see that you (the ex-victim) no longer deserves to be held hostage by the pain of a situation over which you had no control?

Can you further see that this situation had nothing to do with whether or not *you* were worthy? Expect to see these things and you will. Allow for them *because they are true!*

Can you also see that even though you may have "the right" to be upset, there's absolutely no value in holding onto this incident or considering it proof of anything? Can you also see that this incident has been taking up far too much space and energy in your life? Are you finally willing to give it up forever?

If so, close your eyes and visualize the bad trophy you earned for this incident crumbling into tiny pieces - and watch as those pieces disintegrate into dust – and then be empowered as this dust is blown away by the breath of the Divine Spirit.

At last, give yourself a good trophy for letting go (add it to the list from exercise #3) and then repeat this process for each incident you are prepared to forgive.

"To be wronged is nothing unless you remember it."
-Confucius

Finally, go back to this list and over-write each entry with the phrase: ***I am worthy – I forgive.*** As you write these words, let go of any lingering negative emotion by allowing yourself to feel empathy for whomever it is you need to forgive, as well for as yourself.

In the end, reflect truthfully on each incident to confirm that you are no longer feeling any leftover pain or anxiety (repeat the process for any incident you feel you haven't let go of completely), for at this point, these incidents should exist for you as nothing more than *simple truths.* And while the truth is certainly and simply *what's so,* it is even more simply *"so what."*

"Forgiveness does not change the past,
but it does enlarge the future."
-Paul Boese

Congratulations! Having made it this far, you have obviously finished *reading* the first four Exercises – which, of course, can in no way be confused with having *completed* them. Therefore, I recommend that you not begin the last two chapters until you have begun to observe a significant shift in your behavior as a result of doing the Exercises.

Still, even after completing the first four Exercises and experiencing this "shift," there is an even deeper level of "knowing" to be realized by those who are willing to *stay the course* in pursuit of something *more.*

Therefore (and no matter whether you do so before or after reading the last two chapters), I invite you to "stay the course" by partaking in the following *Advanced Exercises* – which are available for download (free of charge) at www.thetrophyeffect.com:

Advanced Exercises & Practices

Exercise #5: Excellence & Breaking through
Exercise #6: Oneness ("Experiencing Connectedness")
Recommended Practices: Being in Nature, Reflection, Meditation

---

Whether or not you choose to participate in the *Advanced Exercises,* I recommend that you revisit the first four Exercises as often as it serves you to do so – or as follows:

Exercise #1: Every six months, or as desired
Exercise #2: Ongoing - yet I suggest that you review this exercise every six months (including a journal)
Exercise #3: Every three months – *yet why not remain engaged at all times?*
Exercise #4: Gratefulness; weekly (or as often as it serves you)
Forgiveness; every six Months

"Follow effective action with quiet reflection.
From quiet reflection will come even more effective action."

-James Levin

Chapter 20 - *The Divine Game*

"...If you truly want to be happy, get out of your own way! Divorce the past, marry your dreams – and then dedicate your Self to being a hole in the universe through which the Divine Spirit can work its magic..."

-Michael Nitti

Be honest. Have you completed the Exercises – or have you begun this chapter before working all the way through them? If you have skipped ahead, I encourage you to return to the previous chapter and give yourself the gift of experiencing what can only be experienced by *doing* the Exercises. The gift of an incredible shift in how you feel as it relates to "being in the world," – which can only be known on the other side of knowing it. Therefore, if you've not yet completed the first four Exercises, please do yourself a favor and do so before reading any further...

If you did complete these Exercises and remained dedicated to the process of awarding good trophies until this "shift" showed up (including capturing your insights in writing as recommended), then what has likely been revealed to you is your natural ability to create your*Self* at will. And, in the wake of having played full out, there's virtually no way to have done so without experiencing your-self as "whole and complete." In which case, I trust that this truth has been revealed to you as well.

What's more, on this side of having repeatedly and intentionally stepped beyond your fear (especially during the third Exercise, which would have required you to override your mind in the face of it pleading with you not to do so), it's unlikely that you could have stayed the course or brought forth that much courage without having realized that you are, indeed, magnificent beyond your wildest imagination!

So, which is it? Did you honestly play full out – or did you simply *dabble?* Since there is no middle ground, anything other than having participated fully has likely left you with something other than you deserve – in which case, you may have settled for becoming "smarter" when you could have been *transformed.*

On the other hand, if you have done the Exercises but are not quite "feeling it," a more accurate way of expressing this fact would be to acknowledge that you are simply not feeling it *yet* – because you have every ability to continue doing the Exercises until you do come to experience yourself as described above; in other words, *as one with it all…*

You see, it's not about whether you understand the Exercises intellectually, but how you approach them. Given which, it's not only a matter of desire, but a matter of intention. For although you may sincerely <u>want</u> to experience *oneness* and *intentionality*, there is a tendency for human beings to become stuck in the hope that a thing will occur, rather than bringing forth an expectation or intention that it will – which is why you may have been guilty of "dabbling," as opposed to going for it with all your heart.

Yet, if someone is truly committed to something, why would they <u>not</u> be inclined to go for it "with all their heart"? Why would anyone "choose" to dabble?

For the simple reason that if you did play full out and then failed to achieve your goal, it would be impossible for the mind to *justify* why you fell short, which it would consider the ultimate failure! Therefore, your mind will actually do its best to block you from going 100% unless it's convinced that you know what you are doing (as it would prefer that you simply not go for something rather than risk falling short). This is especially true when it feels that you have no clue about what you are getting yourself into, which is precisely how the mind feels about "oneness" or anything else that it doesn't perceive as attainable from its perspective.

The bottom line is that the only way to break free of your personal conditioning or to break through any fear is to play *full out* even as your mind is pleading with you not to. To keep doing the Exercises in spite of your mind imploring you to give up – which you may notice it doing by "subconsciously suggesting" that you settle for an intellectual understanding of the Exercises (as if such an understanding might somehow cause you to experience that which is only attainable by *experiencing* it).

You see, within the context of *The Divine Game**, "understanding" is the "booby prize". No amount of learning can produce such a profound shift in consciousness, just as one cannot master the distinction *balance* by simply reading about how to ride a bicycle. The only way to come to <u>know</u> *balance* is by getting on a bicycle and sticking with it until "balance" shows up.

Likewise, the only way to experience the distinction "transformation" is to keep going for it – no matter how uncomfortable or confused you may become – until you "get it." Consequently, *desire* and *knowledge* are false friends on this leg of the journey…

In recalling the story of my client who had pushed through his discomfort in support of the gentleman with the walker, please notice that this is precisely what transpired in that situation. For in the face of the tug-of-war between him-*Self* and his *mind*, my client stayed the course out of his intention to make a difference and to break through his fear. Being aware that his discomfort would never subside, he chose to step beyond it. He took action in spite of his mind imploring him not to – and with no guarantee that he would experience anything other than the satisfaction of having done so – he refused to quit. Only then, as a result of intention, faith, and determination – did a "Divine shift" occur.

**The Divine Game: the play of life beyond the fishbowl, born of intention, devoid of ego, and practiced in concert with the oneness of the universe.*

-Michael Nitti

In the wake of this incident, my client realized that *he* had been the author of his own experience. His refusal to quit had caused *oneness* to be revealed so profoundly, that he knew that he would never forget it (just as the distinction *balance* can never be forgotten once it shows up). What's more, he was certain that the universe had intentionally steered him toward this circumstance, as it was evident that this incident had to have happened in order for him to be transformed. Still, had my client not been open to any of this (*expecting* it), he'd have probably done nothing more than hold the door for that gentleman on that fateful day.

Yet, how do I know for sure what my client experienced? How do I know for sure what he felt or what he realized to be true or how it impacted his life? Well, I do know for sure because that client was *me.* Literally.

Just as it continues to be *me*, as I am privileged to experience this same sense of Self and oneness whenever I push beyond my mind with the intention to contribute and make a difference.

Ultimately, I realized that the experience of oneness is available in every moment. And although it initially began tapping me on the shoulder over twenty-five years ago (as it did with that gentleman in the restroom – and then as it did when I later rappelled down the face of a mountain – or as it did when I first spoke in front of hundreds of people), it continues to show up just as powerfully when I simply open my heart and allow myself to feel inspired and connected in the presence of another human being – *or* by nature itself…

Of course, there are those who come to experience oneness by practices other than I'm describing here – and certainly without having to learn about the four premises of *The Trophy Effect* before doing so. However, since this book evolved out of the way in which I came to know it (and have since been teaching others to know it), I encourage you to remain dedicated to the path you are on…

Even so, I am certainly not married to my way of teaching, as it is my intention that you come to know oneness by whatever means serves you. Surely, there are methods which are more subtle in their approach and which tend to "cultivate" the experience of oneness over time; thereby inducing the mind to "go silent" by some means other than pushing through fear. These practices include various forms of meditation, as well as "accessing the field of pure potentiality" via spiritual or psychic revelation. What's more, a *Divine shift* may also be inspired by the study of either Psychology or Quantum Mechanics, as the latter offers direct access to the actual science behind "the true nature of things."

Of these practices, meditation is often regarded as not only a "path" but a "means" – which is why I encourage you to meditate regularly in support of remaining heedful of the distinction between your *Self* and the *mind* – as spending time in silence can be both a pleasant and effectual means of surrendering into one's connection with *Source.*

On the chance that you may be interested in exploring these other paths, I have included an addendum with a list of books and programs that will support you in this regard. However, I promise you that no matter how you eventually come to know it, the final step into oneness will ultimately require that you let go of "all that is known" while surrendering into that which is *not*...

In consideration of which, although you may eventually enjoy exploring these other paths (as have I), given that you've already come this far and are familiar with the Exercises, I implore you to remain faithful to the path you are on. After all, for what reason would you want to "sit silently atop a mountain," or otherwise change course, when *The Trophy Effect* has delivered you here?

Being fully respectful of these other disciplines and mindful of those who were ultimately enlightened after seeking the truth by other means – I can assure you that all paths lead to the same truth. To which end, if you truly intend to follow *this* path but have not yet completed the Exercises, I not only encourage you do so *immediately,* but to do so *with all your heart!* Which, I suggest, would be analogous to "charging in through the front door" versus "slipping in through the side door when no one is looking."

Even so, there is no "correct" path – and certainly no guarantee that you will experience a "Divine shift" as a result of doing the Exercises. However, rarely has anyone played full out and not experienced a relatively major breakthrough on some level.

Still, I can assure you that you will never come to know "enlightenment" by simply *understanding* it – as *The Divine Game* can never be "won" by attempting to do so from a purely intellectual perspective. Therefore, I urge you to seek out that which you are afraid of (or that which you avoid) and become friends with *that.* Not for the purpose of understanding why you fear it (or are avoiding it), but with the intention to embrace it and to put it behind you.

In fact, I suggest that you make this a game by seeking out and pushing through all that has stopped you in the past – as well as by doing as many out-of-the-ordinary things you can on a daily basis. Demonstrate to your mind that you are in charge!

For instance, if you typically take a short-cut to work, take a more scenic route. If you normally get up at 7:00 am, get up at 6:30. If you don't usually converse with the passengers on your bus, strike up a conversation with as many as possible (or whatever your metaphorical equivalents of these activities may be). Notice what it is that you avoid and then be willing to no longer avoid it.

Remain on the lookout for as much evidence as you can find of our collective magnificence – and be sure to follow up any trophies you award to others with a vocal acknowledgment as well. For example, if you observe someone refilling a copy machine with paper or making a fresh pot of coffee after pouring the last cup, put your appreciation "on loud speaker" with the intention that they get it.

No matter how insignificant an incident may be, permit yourself to be inspired and then "pay it forward" at every turn – allowing yourself to feel as connected as possible to those with whom you are interacting. Observe their desire to make a difference and notice that it is no less intentional than your own. Notice how others are pushing through their fears as you would push through yours. Be willing to disregard anything that has happened in the past and simply "be" with people. Be with *who* they truly are and not with who you've *assumed* them to be – and then award trophies to everyone involved.

Ultimately, expand your consciousness. Look for evidence of our individual and collective magnificence in everyone and everything. Observe people being great. Appreciate all that others have accomplished. Spend time in places where people put their magnificence on display. Museums. Theatres. Libraries. Concert Halls. Sports arenas. *Be* with all the art and all the books. *Listen* to all the music. *Watch* all the athletes and entertainers excel! If you were to spend a couple of weeks doing all of these things it would be very difficult *not* to acknowledge our collective magnificence. Therefore, do this as often as you are able – and expect to see the truth.

And yet, the truth reveals itself only to those who are *looking* for it; not to those who are expecting to see something other than oneness and magnificence. Nor will the truth be revealed to those who simply "hope" that they will see it. In fact, there is no need to hope that something will occur when you are *expecting* it to! No one has ever sat atop a mountain for any length of time "hoping" to be enlightened, as remaining devoted to any such outcome requires an intention, born of an expectation, and accompanied by faith.

Therefore, allow these Exercises to be your mountain – yet do not attempt to "climb it" *hoping* that you will attain anything. Instead, allow faith to be your guide – and then take each and every step with the expectation and intention that you will be transformed.

Finally, after completing all six Exercises, I recommend that you continue to engage in the "Recommended Practices" as often as it serves you to do so; always expecting to see the *Divine Spirit* in everyone and everything. In time, you will realize that there is nothing to prove and that we are all *one with Source*. And, as you come to appreciate that no one is inherently greater or lesser than anyone else, what will follow is the ability to appreciate and celebrate everything that may have been accomplished or acquired by other people – including what others may have learned or become as a result of having stepped beyond *their* fears.

Be willing to allow any jealousies to drift away. Allow yourself to "be one" with those who you consider to be extraordinary, as well as with their accomplishments. Celebrate those accomplishments as you would your own. Share in them. And then go out and do the best you can at what you do – knowing that you are doing so on behalf of everyone else. Contribute your magnificence to the universe. Know that you are part of "the collective magnificence" and then give yourself a trophy!

The Divine Game challenges us to bring forth our magnificence because we can – not in order to prove that we are good enough or to dominate anyone else with our "personal" greatness. That is a mind game – a game that can't be won – because it simply triggers other minds to do the same. Therefore, refuse to play that game. And yet, what is life if not a game? Competing against oneself and others is a worthy and joyful pursuit when the intention is to win by *excelling* rather than by *domination.* The spirit demands that there be soaring. Thus, it is our birthright to excel and to be all that we can be.

As you are able to honor your own magnificence, I invite you to observe and honor this in others as well. Although "*who* we are" is fundamentally inseparable, within the context of our "human experience," each of us has been blessed with the freedom to pursue various courses of study and the ability to nurture "personal" gifts or talents, which some of us are able to manifest and express at higher levels than others. Therefore, even as you play at your highest level, you are sure to encounter those whose "higher level" may be higher than yours – and the inclination to measure ourselves against one another is simply part of "the game." Even so, winning or losing is *never* a measure of one's inherent magnificence, but a measure of how well one has mastered a particular *human* game.

However, at the level of *The Divine Game,* once you have surrendered into the truth of your connectedness with everyone else, no matter what human game you are playing or with whom you are playing it, there is no way you can lose. Consequently, if *you* win, you win – and if "they" win – you win!

Even if you are in direct competition with others (perhaps as a member of a sports team or a sales force, or otherwise feel that you are in a position to have your performance compared with that of others on a regular basis), do not allow either the fact that you have outperformed someone else or the fact that you may have been outperformed to dissuade you from being inspired by what has been accomplished by you or anyone else. Do what you do to the best of your ability, yet observe and acknowledge where others are excelling as well – and then be sure to award lots of trophies.

As an expression of your connectedness to everyone and everything else, allow yourself to be inspired by these *individual* expressions of our *collective* magnificence. Some of us are excellent athletes, musicians, or artists. Some of us are outstanding teachers or sales people or leaders in the community. Some of us are lauded scholars or philosophers, while others allow their intention to manifest as mothers or fathers or as counselors of others. The truth is that no matter what paths others have taken, "that" which is flowing through *them* is identical to "that" which is flowing through *you.* Therefore, celebrate this with all your heart and then allow "it" to flow through you as fully as possible, for that is the grandest expression of who you are!

"This is the true joy in life - the being used for a purpose recognized by yourself as a mighty one; the being a force of nature instead of a feverish, selfish, little clot of ailments and grievances complaining that the world will not devote itself to making me happy. I am of the opinion that my life belongs to the entire community and it is my privilege to do for it all that I can...

Life is no brief candle to me, but a sort of splendid torch, which I have hold of for the moment and I want to make it burn as brightly as possible before handing it on to future generations...

- George Bernard Shaw -

Chapter 21 - *Life Beyond the Fishbowl...*

"There is no passion to be found in playing small –
In settling for a life that is less than you are capable of living."
–Nelson Mandela

Exuberant. Free. Connected. Joyful. *Rejuvenated...*

So, how many of these words describe you now that you've left your fishbowl behind? Most of them, I would expect. Yet, whether you're "feeling it" now or not, I implore you to continue doing the Exercises until you've broken totally free of your old conditioning. In other words, until you are no longer inclined to award yourself *bad* trophies and have become a master at passing out *good* ones…

Typically, it takes several weeks for any such re-conditioning to take effect. During which time, the actual neural-connectors within your brain will begin to "re-wire" based on how you are *being,* as your mind begins to align with what is actually occurring and working in your life. Which is why it is essential that you *do* the Exercises (rather than simply understand them) and why it's especially important to celebrate with good trophies.

Even so, I suggest that you let go of any hope that *intentionality* might ever occur by default, as your mind will forever be inclined to react instinctively to any situation it perceives as a threat. However, now that you are aware that this is occurring, you will be empowered to react consciously rather than defensively. And although the very nature of "intentionality" prevents it from ever showing up automatically, there is nothing to prevent you from overriding your mind *on purpose* – which means you will always be able to do so *at will!*

As you are able to "react intentionally" (hence, as the "author of your own experience"), you will ultimately come to see the reflection of your magnificence in everyone and everything. You will come to be enlivened by the associated feelings of connectedness and love, as you stand in the truth of your oneness with the universe. This is your birthright. And it all awaits you *beyond the fishbowl!*

In light of which, what better way is there to preview "all that awaits you," than by reviewing the various testimonials submitted by those who have previously completed the Exercises? Therefore, I invite you to visit www.thetrophyeffect.com, where I trust that you will not only be inspired by what has already been posted but will be inclined to submit your own testimonials via email. In fact, I suggest that you visit this website as often as possible for the purpose of being empowered – and to empower others – by sharing your personal experiences as well.

Speaking of sharing personal experiences, as you may have assumed, my personal Bad Trophy Room has been "boarded up" for quite some time. Yet, in fact, I can clearly recall the very day I shut it down so many years ago. Having taken pause to lament once more all that wasn't working in my life, I had just begun to feel even sorrier for myself than usual, when – incredibly – my Bad Trophy Room both came and went in the blink of a divine eye!

By that time, I had been "seeking the truth" for several years and, having recently realized that I was asking myself the same old disempowering questions (Why me? Who's to blame? – etc.), I had finally begun to think "outside the fishbowl." Even so, up until that moment, I had only entertained this concept *intellectually,* as I still didn't "get it." However, on a remarkably clear day in Seattle, a mere two weeks after assisting that gentleman in the restroom, I was struck absolutely speechless by a glorious epiphany!

In that moment, "the lights came on" and the *pity-party* was over for good! And where do you suppose I found myself when the lights came on? That's right – in the *Bad Trophy Room* – where I was being treated to a movie-like "re-run" of every event in my life that had ever caused me pain. What's more, I not only recognized these negative events (which I had intuitively perceived as "trophies") as the source of *all* my suffering, but could clearly see that: ***a)*** these events were living as proof that I wasn't good enough, ***b)*** I was fully responsible for how I interpreted these incidents and how I felt about them, and ***c)*** if I hadn't witnessed what I did, I would have likely continued to dwell on these things for the rest of my life!

Needless to say, this was a very "enlightening" revelation. And yet, it was the next realization that transformed my life; which was that it didn't have to be this way! That I had the power to do something about it!! At which point, that's precisely what I did – for within little more than an hour of becoming aware of its existence, I closed my Bad Trophy Room down *forever*...

Within that blessed hour, I found myself delivered by a higher consciousness to a place that was both "everywhere and nowhere," from which I was privileged to experience my oneness with the entire universe. I was transformed by the grace of the Divine Spirit and the love that was clearly flowing through me, as it was flowing through *everything.* What's more, I could see that everything was whole and complete, just as it was – and that all that ever was, *always* would be. I was present to the truth – and I was grateful. And with that, my Bad Trophy Room faded away, and *The Trophy Effect* was born…

Yet why are you only hearing about this now, more than twenty-five years later?

Frankly, it's because I have been "thinking about" writing about it for several years – all the while wondering how to impart it effectively and in some manner other than by simply "explaining" it. Certainly, I was aware of the power of *The Trophy Effect* in that it had changed my life so profoundly – and has since changed many others. In fact, it was within weeks of discovering this dynamic that I began to apply it in working with many of my earliest clients; typically supporting them in overcoming what they had previously believed to be insurmountable roadblocks to their success.

And still, it's been a fairly well-kept secret until now. Of course, I certainly didn't write this book with the intention of keeping it a secret any longer. So, now that you know *the secret,* what are you going to do with it?

Well, whatever you do, I invite you not to settle for anything less than you deserve. Therefore, once you finish reading the following segments on "Focus," "the Four Premises," "Now," and "Alignment," I encourage you to keep doing the Exercises until you find that you actually are passing out good trophies like door prizes!

The Power of Focus

Now that you know that your fear of not being good enough stems from the fact that you've been carting around a Trophy Room full of evidence that it's probably true, what is it that *specifically* causes this fear to show up when it does? Could it be that there's simply no way to avoid thinking of such things when they lay no further than a single, "self-deprecating thought" away?

Well, if proximity was to blame, since you've lived your entire life within "thinking distance" of your Trophy Room, you would have always been present to this concern. Yet, no matter how often you may have felt this fear, it wasn't *all* the time. Thus, it's evident that the only time you were ever influenced by your bad trophies is when you *focused* on them. In other words, you never lamented these trophies simply because they existed, but because you *did.* You focused on your bad trophies! In which case, one could argue that you've never really had a "Bad Trophy Room issue" – you've had a "*focus* issue."

Basically, "focus" is that which gives rise to all that we might ever be, or have. Good or bad. If you focus on things that cause pleasure, you'll get pleasure. If you focus on things that cause pain, you'll get pain. It's a pretty simple equation. Consequently, if you focus on something you want – and then remain focused on it – you will very likely get it. On the other hand, if you focus on what you *don't* want, you'll likely get that instead. Therefore, and as you can see, being careful with regard to what one focuses on is no small consideration.

Given which, although you've already sworn off awarding yourself bad trophies and promised to stay out of your personal Bad Trophy Room altogether, the truth of the matter is that our *collective* Bad Trophy Room is overflowing with some pretty horrific incidents (I challenge you to watch any daily news program and then not acknowledge this as true). Therefore, in support of maintaining a positive psychology in the face of so much global negativity, it will serve you to both understand and master the "power of focus."

Quite simply, the power of focus is the force behind accomplishing anything you want to accomplish in life. It is the very "fuel" behind the *Law of Attraction,* as you wouldn't be able to move – or be drawn – toward any meaningful goal or outcome without it. On the other hand, *focus* also fuels the *Law of Aggravation**, in that it is just as easy to be drawn toward your *distractions.* For instance, if you focus on a particular concern that something may prevent you from achieving an outcome, you will be drawn toward that concern rather than toward what you set out to achieve – unless you consciously shift your focus away from that distraction and back toward your outcome.

No matter what outcome you may be pursuing or how much aggravation you hope to avoid, you and I have been blessed with the ability to shift our focus at will. Of course, you may not feel like you possess this ability, because most of us can recall situations when we attempted to shift our focus but then gave in to a distraction or a concern anyway. Still, if this has happened to you, what occurred in those situations is not proof that you lack this ability. It's simply proof that you got distracted – and then *got stuck...*

*The Law of Aggravation: If you focus on something that is able to thwart your intention, *it will.*

Simply put, life includes distractions. Many of which you or I might otherwise be inclined to enjoy as *diversions* if or when we had nothing better to do. However, as ironic as it may be, these very same diversions are routinely utilized by the mind as distractions (a dynamic commonly referred to as "procrastination"), which it dangles cleverly before us in its attempt to prevent us from playing full out (which you now know that it does in order to prevent you from failing without being able to justify why you failed).

Indeed, we all get distracted at times, for who hasn't played a video game or watched TV when they should have been studying? Who hasn't excused themselves to answer a cell phone during a meeting or surfed the Internet in lieu of working on an important project? Of course, there are times when we give in to these distractions willfully; yet, unless you've planned your day around them or have otherwise decided to engage in these activities as diversions, they will likely compromise your effectiveness by throwing you off course (which, in the past, would have caused a fair amount of upset and likely earned you a bad trophy)...

"The only difference between a diversion and a distraction is whether you scheduled it or it scheduled you."

-Michael Nitti

As you come to gain mastery over *The Trophy Effect*, you will find that you are increasingly able to maintain your focus in the face of whatever the mind dangles before you. Whenever a distraction (or fear) shows up, your objective must be to allow for it, handle it or dismiss it, and then return your focus to whatever you were doing before you got distracted; thereby re-directing your attention from the distraction (or fear) and back toward your outcome.

In order to meet this objective, you must shift your focus *away* from the distraction without making the distraction "wrong," wishing it hadn't occurred, being upset about it, or otherwise "granting it

Power" – as this would be akin to focusing on it (hence, you'd be drawing your attention right back toward it). Therefore, the secret to effectively re-focusing away from any distraction or challenge is to focus on the *resolution* of that challenge (rather than on the issue itself) while never losing sight of your original outcome.

Ultimately, the key to taking full advantage of the "power of focus" is to know exactly *what* you want and *why* you want it. You must define your purpose and your outcome as clearly and completely as possible. In fact, when it comes to focus, there is no such thing as too much clarity. Given which, if you are interested in learning even more about this topic, I highly recommend that you read "The Power of Focus," by Jack Canfield, Mark Victor Hansen, and Les Hewitt. A book that leaves absolutely no stone unturned...

"Focus on where you want to go, not on what you fear."
-Tony Robbins

Exercising Autonomy Over the Four Premises of *The Trophy Effect*

As if dancing subconsciously to forces orchestrated by our cultural conditioning, our lives have been choreographed by an assortment of fear-driven considerations, notions, and beliefs; which have caused us to not only discount our self-worth, but to settle for far less than we deserve. And although I have faith that you are already feeling more empowered after completing the Exercises, I leave you with the following four summaries, which offer specific coaching on how to exercise and enjoy greater autonomy over each of the basic premises of *The Trophy Effect*...

Premise # 1

Whenever you arrive at a moment of decision, you cannot help but be influenced by *all* the trophies in your Bad Trophy Room, which is where the mind delivers you anytime you feel a fear associated with contemplating an outcome. Hence, ***all of your important decisions are made in the shadow of your bad trophies!***

Counter Action:

Quite simply, don't do this. Do not contemplate any course of action while lamenting anything about your past.

Instead, put yourself in a resourceful state, create an empowering atmosphere, and surround yourself with trusted advisors. Weigh the "pros and cons" and resist any urge to make snap judgments. Does it ever make sense to think back on situations that didn't go as planned? Absolutely – especially if you are contemplating a similar course of action – as it will surely serve you to learn from any past mistakes. Yet, it will also serve you to acknowledge the differences between then and now. Ultimately, once you decide to move forward, you must be clear about your outcome, *expect* to succeed, and celebrate every little win along the way with a good trophy!

Premise # 2

That as a result of both your fear of not being good enough and your culturally-driven inclination to remain humble, you have been living with your "finger on the mute button" – therefore you have not been inspired to fully acknowledge yourself and others. For this reason, ***as bad as you may feel about all the negative trophies in your Bad Trophy Room, it's likely that you feel even worse about the lack of trophies in your Good Trophy Room.***

Counter Action:

This resolution is equally as simple, as the best way to 'take your finger off the mute button" is to fill your Good Trophy Room as full as possible, as soon as possible, and then never stop! Therefore, it's imperative that you let go of any lingering resistance you may have to self-acknowledgment. If you have no desire to "blow your own horn" publically, then don't, but if you fail to acknowledge your inherent magnificence, you will also fail to unleash your full Self. Again, it's *fear* that's been holding you back, not humility. Therefore, embrace your magnificence and your power! In the end, if you prefer to go forth quietly, that is up to you – but I assure you that there is a lot more joy to be had by going forth *fully*.

Next, you must totally re-invent your evaluation criteria, thereby "freeing yourself" to award all of the good trophies you possibly can. And since I'm the coach, in support of demonstrating how this might look, I offer the following example of one of my typical daily routines:

> Get up early; *trophy!* Reach down and pet my dogs (two dogs); *two trophies*. Great workout; *trophy. Really* great workout; *two trophies!* Clear my emails; *trophy.* Respond to a client with an inspiring email; *trophy!* Call my mother; *trophy.* Conduct an outstanding coaching call; *trophy.* Follow it up with a *phenomenal* coaching call; *two trophies!* Write another page in this book; *trophy.* Acknowledge or compliment my wife; *trophies for each of us.* Observe myself awarding trophies; *trophy!!*

For most people, this is no small departure from their usual way of construing things – which is why I have no trouble appreciating it when one of my clients admits to feeling "uneasy" about awarding themselves trophies for anything so trivial (their point being that, by doing so, they would compromise their otherwise high standards). In response to which, I applaud both their intention *and* their high standards.

As a coach, I would never suggest that anyone *lower* their standards. However, I do support you in letting go of your inclination to perceive your life from the perspective of "either / or." Again, the consideration that you are merely entitled to "one or the other" is a *cultural notion* that is likely inhibiting your experience of abundance elsewhere in your life as well – so why wait any longer to give it up?

The truth is that you have every right to award yourself good trophies for anything at all *without* compromising your standards to any degree. Therefore, I encourage you to let go of this notion right now – and then give your-self a trophy for not otherwise lowering your standards!

Remember, one of the major objectives in awarding good trophies is to establish positive neural-pathways within your brain. Previously, you and the door guard had pretty much "worn out the carpet" leading into "your" Bad Trophy Room, which resulted in the construction of a virtual superhighway of neural-connectors leading into that room, while "the carpet" leading into the Good Trophy Room hardly ever got dirty!

Therefore, I invite you to begin *wearing out the carpet* leading into the Good Trophy Room by awarding as many good trophies as you possibly can; thereby creating an entirely new network of neural-connections leading into this room. Once you do, you'll find it practically impossible to stay out of the Good Trophy Room, even if you try.

What's more, by intentionally avoiding the Bad Trophy Room, the neural-connections leading into that room will eventually atrophy from lack of use, which means that although you may not be able to close this room down, you will be able to "replace the worn out carpet" that welcomed you back so often! In any case, the surest way to create new neural-pathways that serve you (while ensuring the demise of those that don't) is to keep doing the Exercises!

Premise # 3

That you do not take *good things* for granted and likely share in the cultural notion that happiness can be attained only as the end result of some form of pursuit or by engaging in special activities. Therefore, ***you have been socially-conditioned to believe that good trophies are very rare and should be awarded only in recognition of something extremely special.***

Counter Action:

For perhaps the first time ever, I suggest that you ask yourself what it takes "to make you happy." What are your "rules" for feeling happiness or experiencing passion? Please revisit Chapter Fifteen and re-read the passages about social conditioning and then notice your own conditioning at play. As you do, I invite you to identify any subconscious decisions that may be putting a damper on your aliveness – and then let them go!

Life is beautiful. You and I are magnificent. Love is everywhere! Still, in order to experience greater joy and passion, you must acknowledge that you possess the ability to "create" these things yourself – and then *expect* that you will do so!

Certainly, I'm not suggesting that certain activities are not more enjoyable than others or that *happiness* and *passion* aren't special. In fact, I consider them very special. Therefore, I would never reserve "feeling them" for special occasions. Again, this is not about *lowering* your standards. It's about *raising* your consciousness to the extent that you are able to generate happiness and passion *at will* – just as you are able to "generate" good trophies at will. Thus, the surest path to happiness is to "steer clear of your fishbowl" while awarding as many good trophies as possible!

Premise # 4

That you already possess the ability to "let things go" and that this ability, when applied in conjunction with the first three premises, ***is the basis from which you will be able to evolve a more self-forgiving and positive psychology.***

Action:

If you are able to master anything at all, master *letting things go*. To which end, I encourage you to apply the "Forgiveness Process" on any issue that you are still holding on to – as often as you need to do so! If you have been unwilling to let go of a specific incident, be honest about w*hy* that is and then do the process on that reason.

Most often, any unwillingness to "forgive and forget" is tied to a memory of having been "done to" (victimized) and a belief that you would feel victimized yet again if you simply let that go. Still, even if you have been victimized, it will serve you to declare that you are done being right about it. More than likely, you are right, so simply appreciate "being right" one last time and then *let it go!* As the author of your own experience, you must take anything you are holding onto and write it out of your script.

Ultimately, although no one would blame you for not forgiving a specific injustice, whatever you are unwilling to let go of prevents you from experiencing your true magnificence. Therefore, let things go! Not because you should, but because you can. Give yourself the gift of letting go – and then honor your-self with an especially magnificent trophy for doing so…

The Power of *Now* – Appreciating the Journey as well as the Destination

In light of the fact that so much of this book has been about focusing on "good incidents" rather than on "bad incidents" and on *outcomes* rather than *fear,* it may appear that what is being implied is that the secret to being happy is to focus on something other than where one happens to be "in the moment." Certainly, it will serve you to focus on *where you are going* rather than on *why you may not get there*. However, this does not mean that life is *about* the outcomes or that you are doomed to be less than fulfilled unless or until you *attain* those outcomes.

In actuality, neither *the journey* nor *the destination* is more or less important than the other. No matter where you've been or where you are going, "now" is all there ever is – as both the past and the future are *illusions.* Given which, within the process of moving toward a particular destination, it could be said that life is nothing other than a series of consecutive "moments of now." Which would confirm that *now* is all there ever is; followed by another *now,* and then another *now,* and so on... Obviously, if you subscribe to the illusion that happiness is dependent upon reaching a specific destination, you would be overlooking an entire series of *moments of now* for the sake of one final moment. Which, I suggest, is not a wise trade, nor one that would support you in "being" fully present.

Therefore, celebrate them all! Bask in the magnificence and the truth of *every* moment. There is no value in looking past one moment to the next – for I assure you that the next moment will arrive when it should. Therefore, simply "be" with the moment you are in. Frankly, I could write volumes on this topic, as it could easily be expanded into an entire book. Thankfully, such a book has already been written – so rather than expose you to any more of my ramblings on the subject, I encourage you to read "The Power of Now" by Eckhart Tolle. For his "ramblings" are truly enlightening.

The Power of Alignment and Intention

Finally, I encourage you to invent a powerful purpose and then embrace it with all your heart! Become fully engaged. Expressions of magnificence are everywhere. There are innumerable individuals and organizations dedicated to making a difference on the planet. Therefore, seek out that which "speaks to you" and make it your own. Be a demonstration of it. Become an "agent of intention." Refuse to live *in reaction.* Focus on your dreams and how you intend to achieve them. <u>You</u> – not your mind – are now in charge of your psychology. Create a Life Plan* that supports you in sharing all of your personal gifts and talents with the universe. Be willing to acknowledge where you've been settling for "somewhat happy" and then make "joy" and "passion" your new best friends!

* Please see page 198 for instructions on how to create a Life Plan

Read books that reinforce these truths. Find a mentor or hire a coach. Identify a role model. Align with those who are on a similar path and honor that in *them,* which is also in *you.* Surrender into your "oneness" with their intention and their purpose, allowing this to empower you, as you, in turn, empower others.

Stay the course! Your mind will surely yearn for its Bad Trophy Room and its fishbowl. It will attempt to lure you back in. Do not allow this to happen. Make the Good Trophy Room your new home. Celebrate your magnificence and give it away. Take your finger off the "mute" button! Love and play full out. And no matter what you do or where you go – *go first...*

"Wherever you go, go with all your heart..."
-Confucius

About The Author –

Michael Nitti is an acclaimed Life Coach and spiritual teacher, who has been touching peoples' lives, as well as their hearts, for over a quarter of a century. Although he is acknowledged as a premier coach for one of the top coaching companies in the world and has held executive level positions in several industries, most of what Michael learned and now teaches came as a result of over thirty years of intensive Transformational course work and study. After participating in his first course in 1980, Michael dedicated himself to the pursuit of higher consciousness; which, in 1983, at the age of 31, resulted in a profound inner transformation.

After his spiritual awakening, he continued to study the works of other spiritual teachers, during which time he also led courses for *Landmark Education* and began to teach and coach individuals with regard to the distinctions of transformation and non-ego based relationships. Unlike other spiritualists, who often devote themselves to teaching full time after experiencing a similar shift in consciousness, Michael remained dedicated to his career as a business professional, continuing to coach and teach "on the side".

In 1997, Michael was recruited by *Robbins Research International, Inc.,* in San Diego, for the role of Director of Operations. During the next eight years, he was privileged to serve as a member of Tony Robbins' Executive Team, where, in addition to traveling the world in support of Robbins' extraordinary events, he was able to sharpen his coaching skills by working so closely with Tony (the "founding father of coaching") himself; eventually serving as a Vice President for RRI before transitioning into coaching full-time in 2005.

Since then, Michael has been one of the most prolific Life Coaches on the planet, coaching an average of 65 to 75 clients per month, which afforded him the opportunity to refine and perfect *The Trophy Effect* (a process he initially created in 1984). Coaching both privately and as a Certified Results Coach with the Robbins organization, Michael specializes in coaching Executives and relationships (with specific emphasis on "honoring the feminine"), as well as training and coaching other coaches. He resides in San Diego with his wife, Julie and is currently in the process of writing several additional books.

"The best way to find yourself is in the service of others."

-Mahatma Gandhi

Note to Psychologists and Life Coaches: If you are interested in being formally trained to lead your clients through *The Trophy Effect* (a training course that will enable you to conduct a 50 minute visualization process, designed to evoke a profound shift in self-esteem and wellbeing), please visit www.thetrophyeffect.com, or contact: training@intentionquest.com.

To learn more about Trophy Effect-related products and programs, please visit; www.thetrophyeffect.com.

If you are interested in personal coaching with Michael, please visit: www.intentionquest.com.

Recommended Programs and Books

Programs & Products:

www.chopracenter.com (Deepak Chopra)
www.waynedyer.com
www.marianne.com (Marianne Williamson)
www.daviddeida.info
www.gangaji.org
www.eckharttolle.com
www.thework.com (Byron Katie)
www.thebleepstore.com (What the Bleep do we Know?)
www.onenessnorthamerica.org
www.landmarkeducation.com (The Forum)
www.tonyrobbins.com (Robbins Research International)
Tell them I sent you: Products; julien@tonyrobbins.com
Programs; erican@tonyrobbins.com
Coaching; steveb@tonyrobbins.com

Books (Higher Consciousness):

Power, Freedom, and Grace; Deepak Chopra
The Spontaneous Fulfillment of Desire; Deepak Chopra
The Diamond in Your Pocket; Gangaji
You are That; Gangaji
Freedom & Resolve; Gangaji
The Power of Now; Eckhart Tolle
A New Earth; Eckhart Tolle
The Power of Intention; Wayne Dyer
You'll See It When You Believe It; Wayne Dyer
A Return to Love; Marianne Williamson
The Gift of Change; Marianne Williamson
Conversations with God: Neal Donald Walsch
A Thousand Names for Joy; Byron Katie
Loving What is; Byron Katie
Awakening the Buddha Within; Lama Surya Das

Books (Transformational / Motivational / Inspirational):

Get Off Your "But"; Sean Stephenson
Awaken the Giant Within; Anthony Robbins
Feel the Fear and Do It Anyway; Dr. Susan Jeffers
The Power of Focus; Jack Canfield, Mark Victor Hansen, Les Hewitt
The Success Principals; Jack Canfield & Janet Switzer
The Platinum Rule; Dr. Tony Alessandra
The Secret Code of Success; Noah St. John
Having it All; John Assaraf
Life's Golden Ticket; Brendon Burchard
Happy For No Reason; Marci Shimoff
Your Destiny Switch; Peggy McColl

Please see the author's website for additional recommendations

How to Create a Life Plan:

Please visit: www.intentionquest.com / About Michael / Life Plan

The Authors Websites: www.intentionquest.com (www.mnitti.com)
www.thetrophyeffect.com

Quotations *from the* Text

Are you willing to see that it is the belief (hence, the expectation) that life's most pleasurable experiences are both sacred and scarce that renders them less attainable?

You have been given the gift of the universe but have refused to accept it, saying instead, "no thanks, I'll just have this little piece of something I'll call me."

Any and all actions that are other than in alignment with pure intention are acts that are perpetuated from the hallucination that you are separate from Source and everything else. In the shadow of any such actions, you will feel alone and you will feel fear; the fear that you're not good enough

As an expression of its intention to manifest itself, Source yearns to be expressed as fully as possible. Thus, when you embrace your magnificence by acknowledging good deeds, you are aligning with the intention of the Universe and helping it make good on its promise...

Undo your social conditioning and you will see the truth...

You are inseparable from all of the good that has ever occurred.

...at some point you perceived that you were separate from that which was thinking you and assumed yourself to be located within your body, which was being used by that which was thinking you. This is when it all went awry. The moment that "that," which you identified as "you" decided that you were distinct from everything else. The moment you decided that you had a beginning and an end...

Most of us are lying around waiting for Love to show up. Quit waiting. If everyone is waiting, then who is going to go first? Go first.

If you truly want to be happy, get out of your own way! Divorce the past, marry your dreams – and then dedicate your Self to being a hole in the universe through which the divine spirit can work its magic...

CPSIA information can be obtained at www.ICGtesting.com
Printed in the USA
BVOW05s0442030916

460759BV00008B/116/P

9 780982 575536